**PRIMARY
FOUNDATIONS**

Physical
education

AGES 5-7

Pauline Boorman

CONTENTS

Author
Pauline Boorman

Editor
Simon Tomlin

Assistant editor
Roanne Davis

Series designer
Lynne Joesbury

Designer
Rachael
Hammond

Illustrations
Ray and Corinne
Burrows

Cover photograph
Martin Chillmaid

ACKNOWLEDGEMENTS

Gina Macoby Literary Agency for
the use of 'Fish' by Mary Ann
Hoberman from *Yellow Butter
Purple Jelly Red Jam Black Bread*
© 1981 Mary Ann Hoberman
(1981, Viking Press);
Coral Rumble for the use of 'Sea
Snake' from *Creatures, Teachers and
Family Features* © 1999
Coral Rumble (1995, Macdonald
Young Books)

Every effort has been made to
trace copyright holders and the
publishers apologise for any
omissions.

**Published by
Scholastic Ltd,**
Villiers House,
Clarendon Avenue,
Leamington Spa,
Warwickshire
CV32 5PR
Text © 2001 Pauline
Boorman
© 2001
Scholastic Ltd

2 3 4 5 6 7 8 9 0
1 2 3 4 5 6 7 8 9 0

British Library Cataloguing-in-Publication Data
A catalogue record for this book is available from
the British Library.

ISBN 0-439-01841-2

The right of Pauline Boorman to be identified as the Author of this work has been asserted by her in accordance
with the Copyright, Designs and Patents Act 1988.

Introduction

The importance of physical education

'Physical education develops pupils' physical competence and confidence, and their ability to use these to perform in a range of activities. It promotes physical skilfulness, development and knowledge of the body in action. It provides opportunities for pupils to be creative, competitive and to face challenges as individuals and in groups and teams. It promotes positive attitudes towards active and healthy lifestyles. Pupils learn how to plan, perform and evaluate actions, ideas and performances to improve their aptitudes, abilities and preferences, and make choices about how to get involved in lifelong physical activity.' (*The National Curriculum Handbook for Primary Teachers in England: Key Stages 1 and 2*, DfEE/QCA).

At a time when there are real concerns over the low levels of physical activity amongst British school children, when they are becoming heavier and fatter and are leading increasingly sedentary lifestyles, this statement highlights the important contribution of PE, not only to promoting healthy lifestyles but to the whole developmental process.

Movement is probably the most natural and spontaneous learning medium for young children. It capitalises on their inherent playful enthusiasm for active involvement in everything around them. It is indeed the essence of childhood and as such is an essential entitlement for all children and an integral part of a broad, balanced curriculum. Schools alone cannot meet the exercise needs of children, but they do have a responsibility to broaden and extend their physical experiences in a variety of contexts (indoors and outdoors, individually and with others, with a variety of equipment) and to help them to move safely, efficiently, imaginatively and with increasing control.

Movement involves three very different but complementary facets of learning: learning how to move, learning through movement and learning about movement.

Learning how to move

The development of physical literacy enables children to manage the everyday demands of living: to be co-ordinated and skilful, creative and expressive, sensitive and energetic in a variety of gross and fine motor activities. In every lesson, all children should have as much opportunity, experience and practice to develop their confidence and competence in these areas as possible.

It is the physical nature of this mode of learning that gives it its distinct identity and makes it unique in the school situation in the sense of being only specifically addressed in physical education. Yet its impact on all other areas of development of the whole learning process, as recent brain studies suggest, can be inestimable (sitting still is one of the more refined of physical skills).

Learning through movement
Links with other areas of the curriculum

We all learn by doing, and for young children particularly, practical experience is an essential ingredient for involvement, assimilation and understanding and often motivation. Through involvement in physical activities, children are presented with many opportunities to think, plan, remember, discuss, assess and solve problems, make decisions and use their judgement. These are skills that are relevant across the curriculum.

There are many ways of using movement as a way of extending, for example, mathematical, scientific or geographical understanding. It is essential, however, that this is not done in artificial or contrived ways, but in ways that genuinely contribute to understanding in other curriculum areas.

Links with personal and social education

Movement also has the potential for providing, extending and enhancing many activities that make demands on children's personal and social capabilities, for example in situations that call for interaction, sharing, taking turns, leading and following, collaboration, negotiation, responsibility, and use of language. We know that physical activity affects feelings of well-being in a broader

sense, but activities that involve children in working in a group or team are not in themselves sufficient to ensure that children work effectively together. Young children need to be helped and encouraged in their interactions in ways that build on their sense of achievement and develop their self-esteem. It is important to find ways of developing confidence and competence through play and practice, preserving and developing the playful spontaneity of their actions.

Links with literacy and language

Throughout each unit of work, children are encouraged to listen and respond to others and to describe, explain and talk about their ideas and activities using appropriate language and some specialist vocabulary. It should be remembered, however, that physical education is primarily about doing, and opportunities for discussion should be brief and purposeful or take place primarily in the classroom, otherwise children might get bored, cold and restless.

Links with numeracy and science

The activities suggested in this book provide ideas for developing an understanding of shape and space in a practical context, experiencing and coming to understand forces and motion in a meaningful way and developing an understanding of how the body works.

Learning about movement

With the current concern about sedentary lifestyles, increasing obesity and the evidence of many hypokinetic diseases beginning in childhood, there are obvious implications for the primary teacher. The most important aspect of this focus on the body, and how it works, is the notion of a developing health awareness. The aspects particularly highlighted in the National Curriculum are each child's knowledge and understanding of fitness and health and of the effects of physical exercise on their bodies. By raising awareness of the role of physical activity in their lives and helping them towards feelings of satisfaction, exhilaration and fun derived from their sense of progress and achievement in physical education, it is hoped that these activities will encourage participation in the full sense of the word (thinking and doing) and that children can be helped to develop positive attitudes and a commitment to physical activity; to make reasoned, informed, and healthy lifestyle choices.

About *Primary Foundations PE*

Through activities in dance, gymnastics, games and swimming, this book attempts to address the requirements of the curriculum and involve children in movement in a meaningful and practical way. The activities are aimed at involving all children in enjoyable and purposeful physical activity.

The units suggest ideas and detail ways in which practical activities can be developed and enhanced within a unit of work or series of lessons.

For each of the core areas of activity within PE, three aspects have been selected to be developed in greater depth. The chapters suggest alternative activities or develop those outlined in the QCA schemes for dance, gymnastics and games, and the final chapter is aimed at beginners in swimming for those schools who choose to teach it during Key Stage 1. Each unit of work can be used to plan half a term's work for the area it covers: 30–40 minutes' activity per lesson. The units:

● provide a basis for developing and extending physical literacy… enhancing each child's movement repertoire and vocabulary in the core areas
● use a combination of exploratory, suggested, guided and directed activities to enable children to practise and develop their skills
● provide links with other areas of the curriculum.

It is important that the ideas given are seen as example plans. There is a great need for flexibility to suit the particular needs of each class or group. As with other areas of the curriculum, it is important to take account of children's previous experiences, current interests and developmental needs.

You will need to use a range of teaching styles and approaches; balancing activities that may be teacher-directed (as is often necessary at the beginning of a lesson to stimulate and involve the children), with activities in which children explore independently or collaborate with others and work together, gradually taking greater responsibility for their own learning.

The lessons suggested blend some independent choices and directed activities with some challenges and activities to boost confidence. All have the potential for all sorts of learning through movement if one is open to the possibilities. It is hoped that teachers using this book will be able to enjoy the activities with the children: observing, encouraging, teaching and monitoring their progress.

National Curriculum

'During Key Stage 1 pupils build on their natural enthusiasm for movement, using it to explore and learn about their world. They start to work and play with other pupils in pairs and small groups. By watching, listening and experimenting, they develop their skills in movement and co-ordination, and enjoy expressing and testing themselves in a variety of situations.' (*The National Curriculum Handbook for Primary Teachers in England: Key Stages 1 and 2*, DfEE/QCA).

The activities contribute to the attainment target that sets out the development of the knowledge, skills and understanding that children of different abilities are expected to have attained by the end of Key Stage 1. The activities in this book are designed to enhance the requirements of the National Curriculum, and provide examples of ways in which the QCA guidelines can be fleshed out.

Acquiring and developing skills
The units will help children to:
- explore ways of using their bodies in different contexts
- repeat skills, actions and ideas with increasing control, co-ordination and understanding
- practise and refine their actions
- manipulate and handle apparatus and equipment
- develop observation and social skills.

Selecting and applying skills, tactics and compositional ideas
Children will be encouraged to prepare and plan for physical activity by:
- choosing, selecting, adapting, varying and modifying actions and ideas
- remembering and linking together
- inventing and creating.

Evaluating and improving performance
Children will be prompted to:
- discuss what they have done, what they liked and what they might do differently next time
- observe, analyse and appreciate the movement of others
- talk and think about what they have done and what they have achieved during the lessons.

Knowledge and understanding of fitness and health
Children will learn:
- how important it is to be active
- how to exercise safely, for example why we warm up before activity and cool down afterwards
- a greater awareness of how their bodies feel during different activities.

Encouraging independence and personal responsibility
The activities will help children to increase awareness of themselves and others, and develop an awareness of safety.

Inclusion

It is now statutory to provide effective learning opportunities for all children (*National Curriculum*, 'Additional Information for Physical Education', DfEE). Teachers are obliged to:

● consider the full requirements of the inclusion statement when planning for individuals or groups

● take account of children's religious and cultural beliefs and practices, such as allowing leggings for Muslim children but discouraging scarves which can be hazardous

● overcome any potential barriers to learning in physical education (some children may require adapted or alternative activities that have integrity and equivalence to the activities in the programmes of study and that enable them to progress, such as a way of travelling rather than jumping or using a ball with a bell in it for a child who is partially sighted; specific support to enable them to participate in certain activities or types of movement, such as the buddy system, NSA support person; careful management of their physical regime to allow for specific medical conditions such as asthma and epilepsy)

● consider planning – where a support assistant is assigned to a child then they should be involved in the planning of activities

● in assessment, when children follow adapted or alternative activities, judge against level descriptions made in the context of the activities undertaken by the child.

For all children, there is a great need to recognise effort and progress rather than measure them against predetermined criteria.

Safety

Challenge and adventure are natural aspects of children's play. By their nature, many activities are hazardous and involve an element of risk. Such challenges within PE are both stimulating and demanding of each child's initiative, courage and determination, as well as their physical capabilities.

One of the most important priorities is to teach children to recognise and cope with the dangers around them in a constructive and positive way, whether it be raising their awareness of the use of skipping ropes, hoops or bats in a limited space; of others as they move about; sharing the responsibility for using or carrying apparatus; or preparing themselves for activity, for going outside, to the swimming pool or further afield. Simple rules can be discussed and established, with the children becoming fully involved in activity so they understand the need for them.

Trial and error is a necessary part of the learning process, but in the context of physical activity, it can often be a long and painful process. Safety precautions cannot remove all risks, but should eliminate unnecessary dangers. Every opportunity should be used to help children develop a sense of safety, alerting them to ways in which their actions may impinge upon the safety of others.

The health and safety requirements in the current curriculum are quite general, so it is useful to look back on the more detailed requirements of the NCC Physical Education non-statutory guidance, June 1992, which states that within all activities, at whatever stage, 'pupils should be taught to:

● be concerned with their own and others' safety in all activities undertaken

● lift, carry and place equipment safely

● understand why particular clothing, footwear and protection are worn for different activities

● understand the safety risks of wearing inappropriate clothing, footwear and jewellery

● respond to instructions and signals in established routines, and follow relevant rules and codes.'
To these must be added:

● Children should be helped to perform movement safely, for example, resilient landings.

● All equipment should be checked and well maintained.

● Teachers need to be aware of any long-standing or temporary medical conditions which may restrict or inhibit participation.

● Tasks and activities will need to be modified to suit the needs of a particular group or class.

● Everyone should be aware of the safety and first-aid procedures within school.

Whatever the situation or the activity, young children should be able to learn how to move under all sorts of conditions with confidence and self-control, beginning to take care of themselves and becoming aware of their responsibilities towards others. When using equipment, help children to be aware of the space and other people. Young children particularly will be concentrating on what they are doing rather than on others around them.

Planning: phases of a lesson

In school, there are, of necessity, many constraints on the ways in which we can encourage children to be physically active. Often, class size, the space and resources available prevent an individualised approach, so the lessons in this book are set out to follow a common pattern.

Preparatory activities

These include all aspects of planning that involve the children.
● Classroom preparation, for example what to wear and changing routines; discussion of safety codes; organisation of groups; reminders about responsibility for apparatus and how this will be organised; discussion of intentions or related ideas.
● Physical preparation, for example activities that will warm up the body. These need to be purposeful and clearly related to the activities that are to follow.
● General preparation, for example response activities and use of space, listening and responding.

Development

Ideas and activities are then developed in a number of ways designed to engage children in many processes of learning and much physical activity. Through a variety of movement experiences, children can be helped to explore the wide range of possibilities and increase their movement vocabulary. Structured and focused tasks and activities will help to clarify ideas and actions and the main focus will be on helping children to think, understand and make judgements.

Climax

The process of practising, consolidating, selecting and/or combining actions will involve children in choosing, performing or sharing experiences. It may involve a sequence devised in gymnastics, a dance, or a made-up activity focusing on bouncing or passing in games.

Conclusion

This will involve: a calming or concluding activity in preparation for changing and returning to the classroom; a review, discussion or evaluation of activities, in the classroom after the lesson.

Assessment

Although the sequence of progression through the stages of motor development is the same for most children, they do not progress at the same or an even rate, so there will be a wide range of differences in the ways children achieve actions and movements. This is natural, as every child is unique. You will be aware that sometimes, in sheer excitement or in response to the demands of a situation, a child will use inconsistent or less advanced movements. Do not worry. Observe and enjoy the actions of the child and continue to create an atmosphere of success, fun and satisfaction.

Because of the fleeting nature of physical actions, detailed observation of a class of children constantly on the move is difficult. However, it is a good idea for you to get a general impression or overall feel for the class response. Ask yourself questions like:
● How do the children respond and listen to my instructions and suggestions?
● How well do they think for themselves?
● How well do they follow others?

- How well do they combine thinking as an individual with working as part of a group?
- How well do they use the space? (Then think how they could be encouraged to use it better.)
- Are they able to use different directions?
- Are they aware of other people when they do use different directions?
- How well do they sustain energetic activity?

Continual review of the class, with a focus on a few children at a time, is recommended. Try to watch how individual children respond and move. There will be times when you note achievement that is particularly significant and times when you look for specific actions or responses. For example:

- Do they use the whole of the body when required? Which parts could they make more use of?
- How controlled are their movements? In which ways could they refine their movements?
- Can they talk about their own movements or those of others?

At this age, children are often inconsistent in their actions, so be aware that there may be occasions when they substitute one travelling action for another (for example a step down instead of a jump; a bounce-jump instead of a hop).

Dance

- How well do they respond to your voice, the rhythm, sounds or music?
- How imaginative and creative are they?
- Are they achieving the qualities required? When? If not, why not? What might help?
- How well do they use individual body parts? Do they use some parts better than others?
- Do they use different levels of their own volition?

Gymnastics

- How do they use the apparatus? Tentatively? Boldly?
- How inventive are their actions?
- Can they hold still shapes on large parts of their bodies?
- Can they take their weight confidently on their hands as they crawl or walk on all fours?
- Can they choose and repeat their favourite movements or select appropriate actions?

Games

- How confidently do they move about larger spaces and handle different pieces of apparatus?
- How do they stop, start and change direction?
- How accurately can they roll or throw towards a stationary target?

At all times, care should be taken to stress the positive aspects of children's movement and to enjoy and encourage their attempts.

Differentiation

This will mostly be by outcome. Tasks and problems are set which the children explore, investigate, try out, solve or are creative with, whatever their level of ability. Movement tasks and questions are open for interpretation, but limited enough for there to be a clear focus for attention.

Most tasks can also be individualised. Individual challenges can be suggested by you or the children. Additional support can be given, or modifications made, for individuals during the course of each lesson as you circulate and support, encourage, insist or challenge.

Sometimes there will be differentiation by input as you target particular children with special grouping, with suggestions (for example, to make the task easier or more difficult or to add an extra dimension) and with questions that vary in complexity or quality.

CHAPTER 1

Dance

Dance, like language, is present in all cultures, and this chapter contains suggestions to enable every child to develop and express their ideas in movement. Emphasis is placed on encouraging children to move with confidence, often starting with actions that are familiar and that they all can do, then developing the imaginative, creative and expressive aspects of each activity.

Most young children love to move to music and will gradually become more aware of and able to respond to the rhythmic qualities of dance. The appreciation and use of sounds, music and rhythms is an integral part of this process. With varied stimuli and the use of contrasting experiences, children can be helped to clarify and refine their ideas and actions, keeping in time with the accompaniment. As they develop greater control and sensitivity in their actions they will be more aware of themselves and others and of the communicative nature of dance.

The warm-up and preparation aspects include listening and responding to the beat, using individual parts of the body to develop body awareness as well as warming up the body and stretching.

Situations are then suggested to provide a framework for ideas and movements. Highlighting contrasting qualities, for example strong and light, fast and slow, high and low, curving and straight, large and small, will help children to raise their awareness of movement and refine their actions.

Using words to evoke particular qualities in their actions, such as *pounce* or *float*, is an important part of this process. By using the body to express themselves in a variety of contexts, children will be able to develop control and sensitivity. They will need time to explore and play with ideas to develop their creativity and sense the satisfaction from the creation of their own unique movement phrases. It is this process of exploring, creating and then linking actions which is most important, and although there are many opportunities to share and observe each other's ideas, performing to the rest of the group is not necessary at every draft stage.

Describing and discussing what they and others have done will help to develop children's ability to appreciate and improve the quality of their work, but the main emphasis must be the practical participation. Some music pieces have been suggested, but percussion or the use of sounds or words themselves will often be more readily available, simpler and a more immediate way to support children with their dance movements.

The topics chosen for this chapter have been selected to provide examples of the use of words, poems and a story as stimuli for dance for young children. The opportunities they provide will encourage children to respond in ways that will challenge them physically, imaginatively and intellectually and help them to access their feelings. Developing simple body actions into dance-like phrases will help to expand and enrich their experiences.

Each unit contains six sessions, providing approximately 30–40 minutes of activity per session.

Alphabet actions

This unit provides opportunities to explore, practise and refine basic actions of travelling, stopping and gesturing through the use of words; from simple actions like *jog* and *jump* to more precise words like *jagged* or *jiggle*, thus helping to develop both word and movement vocabulary.

Using one letter of the alphabet per session, each of these lessons provides the opportunity to select, use and highlight appropriate qualities. For example, *jagged* – sharp, angular.

The Wizard of Oz

The use of selected parts of the story and some characters from *The Wizard of Oz* provides opportunities not only to explore actions with contrasting qualities, but also to think of ways of communicating and expressing feelings.

Under the sea

This uses poetry to support and enrich movement possibilities. Key descriptive action words from the topic are used to extend and develop both movement and word vocabulary.

Alphabet actions

This series of lessons will help children to experience words in action, which will help both their word and movement vocabulary. Each lesson plan focuses on a different letter of the alphabet, and all actions begin with that letter. The actions have been chosen to highlight some of the five different actions of dance: travelling, turning, jumping, gesturing and stillness or different shapes. Each action word is explored and then developed into a phrase of movement. Some words will need more explanation than others, but through participation in the activities, it is hoped that children will gain understanding of the words and actions involved.

The warm-up activities encourage the children to listen and respond to rhythms, make sensitive use of body parts, and make good use of space, as well as warm up the body.

The development part of the lesson introduces the words and encourages the children to explore and experience the particular qualities of each word.

The climax of each lesson incorporates linking some of the actions beginning with the chosen letter to form a sequence.

Children will not need any specific prior experience of dance to be involved in these sessions, but emphasis on spacing will be important. Ideally, they will have explored some basic ways of travelling such as marching and creeping, taken part in circle games or action rhymes and played games such as 'Musical statues'.

The unit is divided into six lessons, allowing approximately 30 minutes of activity for each session. The unit can be extended using further letters of the alphabet.

Links to literacy are essential. The letter *j* has been chosen to start with because *jump* and *jog* are easily identifiable action words, but the individual lesson plans can be selected to match work being covered in the classroom.

UNIT: Alphabet actions

Enquiry questions	Learning objectives	Teaching activities	Learning outcomes
Can we move using action words beginning with _j_?	• Explore action words beginning with _j_. • Raise awareness of the use of space. • Explore and practise different jumping actions. • Practise jogging in different directions in time with a light, steady beat. • Practise jerking parts and then the whole body strongly or lightly (jiggle). • Explore and practise making jagged shapes. • Combine these actions into a sequence.	Warm-up: practising reaching and swaying; drawing large curving shapes and then straight lines in the air using hands then elbows; drawing a letter _j_ in the air; jumping lightly on the spot. Development: jogging lightly on the spot and in different directions in time with the accompaniment; practising stopping when the music stops ('Musical statues'); jogging in straight lines, in curving lines and in the shape of letters; jogging in the shape of a letter _j_; making different jagged shapes; linking the jog and the jagged shape; practise three big jumps with different shapes and at different levels; practising jerky actions, strongly and lightly. Dance: putting together phrases jogging and stopping in a jagged shape, jumping and then jerking. Cool-down: stretching to draw the letter _j_ slowly and smoothly; curling up to relax.	Children: • understand _jump, jog, jerk, jiggle_ and _jagged_ • respond to a beat • use the space well
Can we move using action words beginning with _c_?	• Explore action words beginning with _c_. • Explore and practise cantering. • Practise creeping in different directions in time with an accompaniment. • Practise closing and curling the body. • Copy a partner's closing actions and curled shapes. • Practise letting the body collapse. • Combine this series of actions into a sequence.	Warm-up: drawing a large letter _c_ in the air; practising moving at different speeds (plodding, trotting then cantering). Development: stretching then closing the body and curling up the body resting on different parts; with a partner, copying stretch, close and curl actions; creeping lightly in different ways and directions; emphasising crouched starting position; developing a phrase; practising collapsing. Dance: matching movement to sounds and practising cantering, creeping and collapsing; putting together in a sequence. Cool-down: drawing a letter _c_ in the air; crouching down to curl up.	• use the space well • understand _creep, canter, curl, crouch, close, collapse_ and _copy_ • remember actions when they combine them
Can we move using action words beginning with _d_?	• Explore action words beginning with _d_. • Explore and practise different ways of dancing, in time with an accompaniment/beat. • Practise darting in different directions. • Practise drifting with the whole body. • Explore and practise dropping parts and then the whole body. • Combine this series of actions into a sequence in threes.	Warm-up: tiptoeing slowly on the spot, and around the hall responding to the changing speed of the sound; practising darting to and fro; drawing a big letter _d_ in the air. Development: describing the darting action; drifting lightly using different levels; making up a dance to popular music; practising suddenly dropping part of the body at a time then the whole body. Dance: in threes, dancing to the rhyme of the three jolly farmers, one at a time then all together – finishing by dropping to the floor. Cool-down: stretching high then slowly drooping heads and other parts to lying position.	• understand _dance, dart, dash, drift, droop_ and _drop_ • respond and dance together in threes
Can we move using action words beginning with _t_?	• Explore action words beginning with _t_. • Practise tiptoeing at different speeds in time with an accompaniment. • Practise turning at different levels. • Practise trembling parts and then the whole body strongly or lightly. • Explore and practise making thin shapes. • Combine this series of actions into a sequence.	Warm-up: drawing a big letter _t_ in the air; tiptoeing on the spot and around the hall using different speeds; playing 'statues'. Development: practising thin shapes using different parts of the body; tiptoeing and stopping in a thin shape; practising different twisted shapes; tiptoeing and turning around; practising turning in both directions and at different levels; trying trembling and developing a phrase. Dance: combining tremble and turn, and repeating phrase; adding tiptoe and stop in a thin shape then add tremble and stop in a twisted shape; practising and refining the actions and showing to half the class. Cool-down: tiptoeing on the spot then tremble and pause, and lying down in a thin shape.	• understand _tiptoe, turn, tremble_ and _thin_ • respond to different speeds • understand the difference between a twist and a turn

UNIT: Alphabet actions

Enquiry questions	Learning objectives	Teaching activities	Learning outcomes
Can we move using action words beginning with *w*?	• Explore action words beginning with *w*. • Explore and practise using different speeds and pathways while walking. • Practise wandering in different directions all over the space. • Practise wobbling parts and then the whole body strongly or lightly. • Explore and practise whirling. • Combine this series of actions into a sequence.	Warm-up: drawing a *w* in the air; walking on the spot then in straight lines at different speeds. Development: practising wandering and wobbling; practising whirling at different levels. Dance: combining a purposeful walk, three wobble phrases, and some slower wandering actions and two whirling turns. Cool-down: drawing a letter *w* in the air with each hand; practising wilting; stretching and wilting, lying and relaxing.	• understand *walk, wander, wobble, whirl* and *wilt* • respond to the different speeds of an accompaniment • understand different pathways for purposeful walk and wander
Can we move using action words beginning with *s*?	• Explore action words beginning with *s*. • Explore and practise different sliding actions. • Practise stamping strongly in time with an accompaniment. • Practise swaying in time to music. • Practise shivering parts and then the whole body. • Explore and practise making stretched shapes. • Combine this series of actions into a sequence.	Warm-up: drawing a large letter *s* in the air; clapping then stamping feet in time to the beat, varying the speed. Development: stretching in different ways; trying different ways of sliding; practising shivering parts of and the whole body and developing a phrase – shivering and stopping; practising shaking the body. Dance: linking phrases of stamping, shivering, stamping and shaking actions; stretching and sliding. Cool-down: swaying in time to the music, stretching and reaching to each side.	• understand *stretch, stamp, stand, sit, slide* and *still* • demonstrate the difference between a shiver and a shake.

Cross-curricular links

English: increasing awareness of the letters of the alphabet; increasing vocabulary of action words and shapes; learning contrasting qualities (for example strongly/lightly; large/small).

Resources

A tape or CD player; *Carnival of the Animals* by Saint-Saëns; some popular music with a regular, rhythmic beat; 'Walking the Dog' by Gershwin; *Greensleeves*; tambourine; bells; triangle; cymbals; photocopiable pages 142–6; paper, drawing materials (optional).

30 mins Can we move using action words beginning with *j*?

What you need and preparation

You will need a tape or CD player; music such as 'Swan' from *Carnival of the Animals* by Saint-Saëns or another gentle, flowing tune; a tambourine; photocopiable page 142, copied onto card and cut out for use as flashcards; paper and drawing materials (optional).

In the classroom, before you begin, introduce to the children the *j* action words that will be used during the lesson: *jump, jog, jerk, jiggle* and *jagged*.

What to do

5 mins Warm-up

Ensure that the children are sitting in a space ready to begin the warm-up. They need space in which to stretch their arms in all directions.

Using some gentle flowing music like *Bamboo Flute*, ask the children to reach up high in the air with both hands and then sway them gently from side to side. Ask them to draw large curving shapes in the air, first with one hand then with the other.

Encourage the children to draw straight lines in the air smoothly and slowly and to watch their hands (from high to low, from one side to the other, diagonally). Repeat, using elbows.

Now ask the children to stand up and to draw the letter *j* in the air, emphasising the straight and the curving parts. Encourage them to make it as large as possible. Check when you model this that the curve of the *j* is the right way for the children.

Ask the children to jump lightly on the spot in time to the beat of the tambourine. Repeat this several times with variations, such as moving to a new spot to jump or jumping to turn around.

Emphasise light, bouncy jumps with bendy hips, knees and ankles.

15 mins Development

Draw the children's attention to the flashcards made from photocopiable page 142. Ask them if they can remember the word beginning with *j* for a light running step.

Tap the tambourine lightly and ask the children to tap their hands in time with the beat, and then to jog (little running steps) lightly on the spot to the same accompaniment.

Encourage them to practise jogging in time with the accompaniment. Keep a regular beat for them to listen and move to, and prepare them to stop by slightly slowing the beat and saying, *A–n–d s–t–o–p*. Play the tapping beat for about 16 beats and then come to a stop. Repeat this phrase several times, encouraging the children to listen carefully and to stop when the sound stops.

Invite them to try jogging in different directions – forwards, sideways and then backwards – ensuring that they look where they are going.

Ask the children to use all the space and to see if they can jog first in straight lines then in curving lines. Still using all the space, tell them to try to jog in the shape of letters from their name.

Now ask them, again using all the space, to try to jog in the shape of a letter *j*. When they have finished one, encourage them to do another, keeping in time with the beat. Advise them to start at the top with a straight line, down to the curving bottom, and then back up to the top to add a dot with a two-footed jump.

Ask the children to jog in and out all over the hall and then to stop when the sound stops, like 'Musical statues' but with no one being 'out'. Encourage them to listen carefully to the music and to keep their steps in time with the beat and to stop when the sound stops.

Using the flashcards, draw their attention to another word beginning with *j* – *jagged*. Show them the word, and then ask them to think about and then make a jagged shape. Ask: *What sort*

Alphabet actions

of shape is it? Ask them how they can make their bodies jagged. Are their limbs sticking out? Are their elbows or knees bent?

Tell the children to link the jog and the jagged shape. Ask them to jog to the tapping of the tambourine and when the sound stops with a bang to make and hold a still, jagged shape.

Let the children try one big, strong jump to the loud bang of the tambourine. Show them the word *jump* on the flashcard and tell them to repeat their jump. Emphasise the big qualities and then, as they practise again, the strong ones. Encourage the use of legs and arms to push upwards or along the ground for distance. Ask them to choose a big jump which goes forwards or a big jump that goes upwards, and to practise doing their jumps to three strong beats of the tambourine (*bang, bang, bang*).

Ask the children if they can think of any other ways in which they can make their jump different. *What sort of shape can you make in the air?* (Look for different shapes – big, small, wide, thin, twisted.) Encourage them to try lots of different shapes, and then to choose two to practise in turn. (*Bang and pause, bang and stop.*)

Now ask the children to try some very low jumps that stay near the ground. (*Tap, tap, tap, tap, tap.*) *Can you do this in a different direction?* (*Tap, tap, tap, tap* in one direction, *tap, tap, tap, tap* in another.)

Again using the flashcards, ask the children to describe a jerky action. Encourage them to think about sharp, sudden, strong, angular movements and then to try jerky actions to the *tap, tap, tap, tap* of the tambourine or to the words *jerk, jerk, jerk, jerk*.

Ask them to try and practise walking jerkily and then to try turning jerkily to the same accompaniment, emphasising the sharp, sudden movements. Stress that you want them to try performing the jerky action lightly, and explain that this is a jiggle.

 Dance

To help in linking some of the actions, ask the children to listen to the sounds you are going to play and respond to them with the *j* actions – the jogging, jumping and jerky movements. Put these phrases together on the tambourine:

● light taps for jogging and stopping – *tap, tap, tap, tap, tap, tap and stop* (twice)
● three strong bangs with a pause between each for three different jumps (twice)
● three short, sharp taps – *tap, tap, tap* or the words *jerk, jerk, jerk* with an especially loud one at the end to encourage short, sharp, strong, jerky movements and a strongly held jagged shape as a finishing position.

Repeat the whole sequence to encourage the children to refine their actions and postures.

Cool-down

Ask the children to find a space again and to reach up high in the air with one hand ready to draw the letter *j*. Draw the letter in the air very slowly and smoothly, sweeping right down to the ground with the curved part of the letter. Ask them to repeat this with the other hand and then return to doing it with the favoured hand.

Ask them to curl up small on the floor like a dot before they return to the classroom.

Classroom review

Encourage the children to recall the words beginning with *j* that they tried during the lesson. Ask them to describe the qualities of the jagged action or draw a jagged shape.

Assessing learning outcomes

Do the children understand the words *jump, jog, jerk, jiggle* and *jagged*? Can they respond to the beat? Are they using the space well?

Follow-up activities
● Produce a piece of writing which incorporates some of the *j* words used in the lesson.
● Encourage children to draw some of the *j* words. Can they graphically illustrate physical movement?

(30 mins) Can we move using action words beginning with *c*?

What you need and preparation

You will need a tape or CD player; a tambourine; bells.

Practise the rhyme 'This is the way the farmer rides'. Copy photocopiable page 143 onto card and cut out for use as flashcards in the hall.

Discuss with the children action words beginning with *c*, especially *creep, canter, curl, crouch, collapse* and *copy* for this lesson.

What to do

(5 mins) Warm-up

Help the children to find a space (away from anyone else) and to stand quiet, ready to begin the warm-up.

Ask them to draw a letter *c* in front of them in the air. Then encourage them to make this bigger, starting high and sweeping down to the ground. Practise this a few times.

Ask the children if they remember the rhyme 'This is the way the farmer rides'. Point out that, in that rhyme, the farmer rides at different speeds. Start by encouraging the children to plod slowly on the spot (then around the room) – *clip clop, clip clop*. Emphasise moving into a space.

Now ask them to run slowly on the spot (then around the room), lifting their knees for a trotting action.

Tell them next to speed up and gently canter around the room. Emphasise good use of space and lifting feet off the ground. Use the tambourine as an accompaniment, accentuating the first beat – *DA da da, DA da da*. Encourage the children to try to canter leading with the other leg.

(13 mins) Development

Ask the children to stretch out with their feet apart and to really open and stretch their arms. Then ask them to close their bodies, bringing their feet and arms together, and then to curl up the body as small as they can. Shake the tambourine while they do this and encourage them to have tucked in all parts of their body by the time the sound stops. (Close and curl, close and curl.)

Ask a few of the children which part of their body they are resting on, then ask them all to think of another part they can curl up on. Repeat the shaking sound as they stretch (this could be along the floor), close and curl. Ask them to choose three different curled shapes to make at the end of each phrase (see Diagram 1). Use demonstrations to illustrate ways of doing this.

Diagram 1

Ask each child to stand next to a person near to them and to number themselves 1 and 2. Number 1 shows their partner one of their ways to stretch, close and curl to the accompaniment

Learning objectives
● Explore action words beginning with *c*.
● Explore and practise cantering.
● Practise creeping in different directions in time with an accompaniment.
● Practise closing and curling the body.
● Copy a partner's closing actions and curled shapes.
● Practise letting the body collapse.
● Develop an awareness of finding and using spaces.
● Combine this series of actions into a sequence.

Lesson organisation
Whole-class discussion; individual and paired performance; teacher-led classroom review with individuals giving feedback.

Vocabulary
creep
canter
curl
crouch
close
collapse
copy

Alphabet actions

and number 2 then copies. They could then try that together and practise it. Then ask them to swap, with number 2 showing their action phrase for number 1 to copy.

Ask the children to find a space on their own again and to show you a starting position to indicate that they are going to creep around the room. Draw their attention to, and practise, a crouched starting position.

To the sound of light bells, encourage them to try a creeping action. Ask them what sort of movement it is. *How are you trying to move? Slowly, stealthily, quietly?* Let them practise in short phrases to the sound of the bells .

Ask the children now to think of, and then try, other ways in which they could creep. Encourage them to use: their tummies, hands and knees or their toes (see Diagram 2); another direction. Ask them to try a different way each time the sound starts. (Creep, creep, cre–e–ep… and pause, creep, creep, cre–e–ep… and pause, and so on.)

Diagram 2

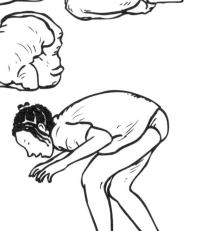

Combine creeping and curling by playing the accompaniment in turn. (Creep, creep, creep and pause, and then curl gradually or quickly up.) Repeat the sequence.

Using the flashcards, ask the children about the word *collapse*. *What does it mean? What sort of action is it?* (A sudden giving way, falling, dropping down.) Ask them to stretch up tall and then to collapse one side of their body as you play a short phrase on the tambourine – strong, short shake (to stretch) and tap-bang (to fall). Repeat this, asking the children to collapse the other side, then the whole of their body. Have fun with this action, but discourage children from falling heavily to the floor. *Coll–apse* could also be used as an accompaniment for this action.

10 mins **Dance**

Ask the children to listen to the sounds you are going to play and to see if they can match the movement to the sounds. *Which is the cantering music? Which is the creeping music? Which is the collapsing music?* Ask them to remember the actions (using the flashcards to reinforce the vocabulary), to find a space and be ready to canter.

Play the cantering accompaniment – *DA da da, DA da da* – several times, and then slow down to prepare the children for a sudden crouch. From this position, ask them to creep, creep, cre–e–ep… and pause, three times, making a curled-up shape at the end of each. From this curled-up position, shake the tambourine for them to stretch out (strong, short shake) and then to choose and practise one way of collapsing to the tap-bang sound. Repeat, emphasising the actions and qualities of the movements (for example light creeping, sudden collapsing). Try this together in sections and then put together a sequence with each child responding individually.

2 mins **Cool-down**

Ask the children to draw a letter *c* in the air, first with one hand then with the other, and then again with the favoured hand. Ask them to crouch down and then curl up on the floor.

Classroom review
Encourage the children to recall the words they have used in the lesson that begin with *c*.

Assessing learning outcomes
Are the children using the space well? Do they understand the words *creep, canter, curl, crouch, close, collapse* and *copy*? Can they remember actions when they combine them?

30 **Can we move using action words beginning with** *d*?
mins

What you need and preparation

You will need: a CD or tape player, popular music with a steady, rhythmic beat; a tambourine; bells; photocopiable page 144, copied on to card and cut out for use as flashcards in the hall.

Discuss action words beginning with *d*. Introduce the words *dance, dart, drift* and *drop* which will be used during the lesson. As a class, practise the rhyme, 'Three jolly farmers' (see Dance, below).

What to do

5 **Warm-up**
mins Ensure that the children are standing in a space ready to begin the warm-up. Ask them to begin by tiptoeing slowly on the spot, then gradually increase and decrease the speed. Then encourage them to tiptoe slowly and quickly as they move around the hall looking for spaces. Try this several times to raise the pulse and encourage the children to listen and respond to the changing speed of the sound.

Tell them to tiptoe slowly on the spot (to the fast shake of the tambourine) and then to dart (tiptoe rapidly in one direction) to a new spot. Then invite them to tiptoe slowly on the spot again and then dash to and fro, looking for lots of new spaces, and to slow down when the accompaniment slows. Practise this, encouraging the children to listen carefully and respond to the sound.

Finally, ask them to stand in a space and draw a big letter *d* in the air, starting at the right-hand edge of the 'circle', going up and round, then high up and straight down to complete the letter.

15 **Development**
mins Using the flashcards, ask the children to describe the darting action (quick movement in one direction), and then to think about the word for slowly moving in one direction – *drift* – that they discussed in the classroom.

See if they can show you a drifting action as they move into a new space. Emphasise the slow, light, smooth nature of this action. Practise smoothly and lightly travelling into a new space, and then encourage the use of different levels (for example drifting from high to low, drifting sideways or drifting from low to high). Use light tinkling bells for the accompaniment.

Ask the children to move their feet and then let them dance to the popular music that you have chosen. For those who need some extra ideas, suggest bouncing, hopping, skipping or turning, trying to keep in time with the beat. Encourage them to try to remember some of their ideas and to repeat them in a phrase.

Tell the children to sink slowly to the ground, then to try again in a sudden movement. Encourage them to try, with the whole body, dropping suddenly to the ground and then to drop just part of the body at a time (for example head, elbows or knees). Play three taps of the tambourine with a pause in between. Ask the children to drop two different parts of their body on the first two taps and then on the last big tap to drop the whole body, and to hold the finishing position in a shape near the floor (such as crouched, lying or kneeling).

8 **Dance**
mins Introduce the rhyme of the three jolly farmers that you went through with the children before beginning the activity:

Three jolly farmers once bet a pound,
Each danced the other one off the ground.

Learning objectives
● Explore action words beginning with *d*.
● Explore and practise different ways of dancing, in time with an accompaniment/ beat.
● Practise darting in different directions.
● Practise drifting with the whole body.
● Explore and practise dropping parts and then the whole body.
● Combine this series of actions into a sequence in threes.

Lesson organisation
Whole-class discussion; individual performances, then performances in groups of three; teacher-led classroom review with individuals giving feedback.

Vocabulary
dance
dart
drift
drop
dash
droop

Alphabet actions

Ask the children to get into threes and to number themselves 1, 2 or 3. Number 1 dances their short phrase, then number 2 dances, then number 3, using the movements they have been practising. Give them an equal length of time to dance, indicating the changes. (The others can tap their feet or clap.) Then ask all three of them to dance together. Give them time to practise this. They could choose to dance their own dance at the same time as the others or work out a way they could dance together, responding to each other (in a circle or in a line; high or low).

In the rhyme, the farmers dance until they drop, so, one at a time, the children should drop, 'exhausted', holding the shape until everyone is down. They may need help with the timing.

Cool-down
2 mins Encourage the children to practise stretching their body up as high as they can reach and then to slowly droop their heads; then droop one arm and then the other; then their shoulders, their backs and their hips. They should be encouraged to continue to the accompaniment of gentle taps on the tambourine until they are lying on the floor. Practise this again to complete the lesson.

Classroom review
As a class or in their threes, ask the children to describe what they did when they danced in threes. *What did you like best and why?*

Assessing learning outcomes
Do the children understand the words *dance, dart, dash, drift, droop* and *drop*? Can they respond and dance together in threes?

30 mins Can we move using action words beginning with *t*?

Learning objectives
● Explore action words beginning with *t*.
● Practise tiptoeing at different speeds in time with an accompaniment.
● Practise turning at different levels.
● Practise trembling parts and then the whole body strongly or lightly.
● Explore and practise making thin shapes.
● Combine this series of actions into a sequence.

Lesson organisation
Whole-class discussion; individual and group performances; teacher-led classroom review with pairs giving feedback.

What you need and preparation
You will need: a triangle; a tambourine; bells; photocopiable page 145, copied onto card and cut out, for use as flashcards in the hall.

In the classroom beforehand, talk about *t* action words, particularly *tiptoe, twist, turn, tremble,* and *thin*.

What to do
Warm-up
5 mins Ensure that the children are standing in a space ready to begin the warm-up. Ask them to stretch one arm up high and to draw a big letter *t* in the air. (Long straight stroke down, then short stroke across.) Let them practise this.

Ask the children to tiptoe on the spot to the sound of the triangle tapping (*ting, ting, ting, ting* and so on). Stress that you want them to move lightly and quietly and then ask them to tiptoe around the hall looking for spaces. Play the *ting ting* sound quite slowly at first and ask the children to try to keep in time with the beat. Then play the sound a little quicker and ask them to tiptoe a little faster as they move around the hall.

Play a game of 'Musical statues', in which the children tiptoe and then suddenly stop. (Nobody is 'out'. Point out that it is not a competition but just to have fun responding to the sound.) Then play the triangle at different speeds, encouraging the children to respond and tiptoe lightly with the appropriate speed of action.

Finally, ask the children to stop in a wide shape when the sound stops. Encourage them to make wide shapes on their feet, on their hands and feet or on a large part of the body.

Alphabet actions

(15) **Development**
mins Invite the children to show you some thin shapes using different parts of their bodies to rest on. Then ask them to tiptoe and stop in a thin shape. Encourage them to make thin shapes on feet, hands and feet or on a large part of the body.

Ask them to stand up and then, keeping their feet on the floor, to twist their bodies around as far as they can to look in another direction. Tell them to try to twist in the other direction. Use a shaking tambourine as an accompaniment. Then together explore other possible ways of twisting the body (lying, sitting, kneeling, for example). The accompaniment should help them to twist and twist and twist and hold.

Ask the children to tiptoe and turn completely around. (Tap, tap, tap and shake/vibrate the triangle.) Practise this together, but do not allow the children to turn more than twice, and when they try again, encourage them to turn the other way.

Ask them if they know the difference between a twist and a turn. (In a twist, part of their body twists to face a new direction; in a turn the whole of the body turns to face a new direction.)

Ask the children to turn around as high up as they can and then to try as low down as they can. This could be a rolling action or turning in a crouched position. (Tap, tap, tap and shake/vibrate the triangle.) Practise this, emphasising the levels. It may be helpful to encourage the children to travel to a new space on the taps of the triangle and to turn at one of the levels as the triangle is shaken.

Using the flashcards, encourage the children to try to remember what *tremble* means and then to have a go at the action to the accompaniment (light taps on the bells). Develop this into a phrase – tremble and pause, tremble and pause. Emphasise the very light shaking action.

(8) **Dance**
mins Combine the instructions to tremble and turn, tremble and turn (the other way) and repeat them several times, encouraging the children to remember the different sorts of turns they could make.

Ask the children to listen to the phrase that you are going to play – tap, tap, tap, tap slowly and pause, tap, tap, tap, tap quickly and pause (tiptoe and stop in a thin shape). Tap, tap, tap and shake/vibrate the triangle (travel and turn, travel and turn, travel and turn). Then shake, shake and shake and bang the tambourine (tremble and stop in a twisted shape). Let the children practise and refine their actions.

Divide the class in two and ask one half, and then the other half, to show each other their sequences. The children could say the words as they see the actions and comment on what they like about the performances.

(2) **Cool-down**
mins Ask everyone to find a space and then to tiptoe on the spot; then to tremble and pause, tremble and pause, then lie down in a thin shape, ready to go back to the classroom.

Classroom review

Ask the children to organise themselves into pairs and to discuss and recall the words they have been using. Ask them to describe the trembling action, then to explain to you the difference between a twist and a turn.

Assessing learning outcomes

Do the children understand the words *tiptoe*, *twist*, *turn*, *tremble* and *thin*? Can they respond to different speeds? Do they understand the difference between a twist and a turn?

Vocabulary
tiptoe
twist
turn
tremble
thin

Alphabet actions

(30 mins) Can we move using action words beginning with *w*?

Learning
objectives
● Explore action
words beginning
with *w*.
● Explore and
practise different
speeds and
pathways while
walking.
● Practise
wandering in
different directions
all over the space.
● Practise wobbling
parts and then the
whole body
strongly or lightly.
● Explore and
practise whirling.
● Combine this
series of actions
into a sequence.

Lesson
organisation
Whole-class
discussion;
individual
performance;
teacher-led
classroom review
with individuals
giving feedback.

Vocabulary
walk
wander
wobble
whirl
wilt

What you need and preparation

You will need: a tape or CD player; a tambourine; music such as Gershwin's 'Walking the Dog'; photocopiable page 146, copied onto card and cut out for use as flashcards in the hall.

Introduce the children to the action words for this lesson, all beginning with *w*: *walk*, *wander*, *wobble* and *whirl*. Introduce or remind the children of the rhyme 'Wibble, wobble, wibble, wobble, jelly on a plate'.

What to do

(5 mins) Warm-up

Ensure that the children are standing in a space ready to begin the warm-up. (They need space in which to stretch their arms to each side.)

Ask them to draw a *w* in front of them in the air. Ask them to stretch up and out to their left to draw a much bigger *w*. Emphasise the straight lines. Then encourage them to travel as they draw the *w*, taking several steps to complete the letter. Repeat.

Tell the children to walk on the spot, and then walk to the tapping of the tambourine in straight lines. If they come near to any other person, tell them to turn sharply to walk off in another straight line so that they are making zigzag patterns on the floor.

Play the tapping sound at different speeds, encouraging the children to listen carefully and to keep their walking in time to the beat. (Strong, slow taps for large, slow strides; soft, quicker taps for shorter, quicker strides.) Encourage good posture with heads up, shoulders relaxed and arms swinging gently by the sides. Help the children to use the space well by praising those who are moving into a space.

(12 mins) Development

Using the flashcards, talk to the children about the word *wander*.
● How quickly do you think you move when you wander?
● How might you move your arms?
● Would you move in straight lines?

Ask them to relax their posture and to swing their arms loosely around them. Then ask them to walk very casually around, sometimes one way and sometimes the other way, making interesting, curving pathways on the floor. Play a light, less regular beat in longer phrases.

Ask the children to try to balance on their toes and then to wobble as if they were nearly going to fall over. Shake the tambourine to accompany this (wobble, wobble, wobble and stop). Ask them if they can remember when they might use the phrase *wobble like a...* Remind them of the rhyme 'Wibble, wobble, wibble, wobble, jelly on a plate', then encourage them to wobble different parts of their body in turn – shoulders, knees, hips – and then the whole body. Encourage them to do this gently, really trying to move the part of the body to and fro, side to side, forward and back.

Make sure that the children are all in a big space and then introduce the word *whirl*, using the flashcards. Ask them to turn around quickly one way (no more than twice in one direction) then the other way, swinging their arms wide. Ask them to try one whirl down low and the next one higher.

(10 mins) Dance

Help the children to combine the actions, starting with the purposeful walk, changing direction after the end of each phrase. (Accompany this with tambourine taps.) Then add three wobble phrases, two using individual parts of the body and one using the whole body (use words – *wobble, wobble, wobble and pause* three times, or a shaking tambourine). Together, practise joining these

two, then add some slower wandering actions (to irregular tapping of the tambourine, or use part of 'Walking the Dog'). To finish the sequence, ask the children to add two whirling turns (with faster shaking of the tambourine).

3 mins Cool-down
Ask the children to draw the letter *w* in the air as large as they can. Repeat several times, alternating hands.

Explain to the class that a word like *droop* that begins with *w* is *wilt*, and that plants wilt when they do not get enough water. Ask the children to very slowly stretch up and then let their bodies wilt bit by bit. Tell them to practise this and then lie down on the floor and relax.

Classroom review
Ask the children if they can remember the words they have been using. Encourage them to describe the actions they have performed.

Assessing learning outcomes
Do the children understand the words *walk*, *wander*, *wobble*, *whirl* and *wilt*? Did they respond to the different speeds of the accompaniment? Did they understand and use different pathways for the purposeful walk and the wander?

30 mins Can we move using action words beginning with *s*?

What you need and preparation
You will need: a CD or tape player; *Greensleeves*; a tambourine; cymbals; photocopiable page147, copied onto card and cut out, for use as flashcards in the hall.

The floor must be clean and clear, particularly for the sliding actions.

Prepare for the lesson by talking about action words beginning with *s*: *stretch*, *slide*, *stamp*, *stand*, *sit*, *still*, *shiver* and *shake*.

What to do

5 mins Warm-up
Ensure that the children are standing in a clear space, ready to begin. Ask them to draw a letter *s* in the air in front of them, emphasising the curving lines. Repeat and practise, making the *s* much bigger, starting high and sweeping down to the ground.

Tell the children to listen to the *bang, bang, bang* of the tambourine and clap their hands strongly in time to the beat. Then ask them to stamp their feet on the spot in time to the same beat. Encourage them to use strong actions, but not to slap their feet on the floor for safety reasons.

Ask the children to stamp as they move about the room. Remind them about keeping in a space. Change the speed of the beat a little and encourage the children to respond by moving more slowly or more quickly as they stamp in time to the beat.

12 mins Development
Ask the children to find a space. Shake the tambourine and encourage them to be in a space when it stops. (They need space in which to stretch their arms in all directions.)

Ask them to stretch out as wide as they can and then to curl up their bodies. Repeat, asking them to stretch out in a different way. Use a shaking tambourine to help the phrasing. Encourage them to reach out right through to their fingertips and their toes. Ask them if their necks and their backs are stretched too.

Learning objectives
- Explore action words beginning with *s*.
- Explore and practise different sliding actions.
- Practise stamping strongly in time with an accompaniment.
- Practise swaying in time to music.
- Practise shivering and shaking parts and then the whole body.
- Explore and practise making stretched shapes.
- Combine this series of actions into a sequence.

Alphabet actions

Lesson organisation
Whole-class discussion; individual, paired or small group performance; teacher-led classroom review with individuals giving feedback.

Now encourage the children to try sliding their feet along the floor as they move to a new space. Then ask them to think of any other ways that they can slide along. Encourage them to use seats, backs or fronts and to practise different sliding actions. Emphasise smooth, continuous movement. Use a gentle cymbal sound as an accompaniment so that the children can be encouraged to keep moving as long as they hear the sound.

Using the flashcards, ask the children to think about the word *shiver*, and when they might feel shivery. Then ask them to shiver their shoulders, then their knees, then their hips and finally their hands to the accompaniment (shaking tambourine – *shake, shake, shake and stop*). Emphasise quick, light, vibrating movements and encourage the children to try just using those parts of the body. Invite them to practise this a few times.

Ask them to try shivering the whole body. Encourage them to keep the movements quick and light. Try shivering and stopping, shivering and stopping, using the accompaniment (shaking tambourine) to provide the phrasing.

Then ask the children to try those actions (shaking parts of the body then shaking the whole body) a bit more strongly to a stronger, louder accompaniment. See if they can feel the difference between a shiver and a shake, and then return to the gentler shivering action.

Vocabulary
stretch
slide
stamp
stand
sit
still
shiver
shake
before
holding

10 **Dance**
mins Remind the children of the stamping actions they tried in the warm-up, and to repeat them to the accompaniment (words: *Stamp and stamp and stamp and stop... stamp and stamp and stamp and stop*; or sound: *Bang, bang, bang and bang and stop*). Then ask them to respond to the shivering accompaniment, choosing two parts of their body to shiver in turn. Repeat the stamping actions and this time on the 'stop', play the stronger shaking accompaniment for them to briefly shake their bodies to. Next, ask them to stretch out slowly and smoothly and move into one of their sliding actions to slide to a new space. Finally, tell them to stretch as wide as they can and then to curl up their bodies quickly before holding still. Repeat, asking them to stretch out in a different way, holding the stretched shape to finish their sequence of movements.

3 **Cool-down**
mins Ask the children to sway in time to the music. Use *Greensleeves* or a similar gentle, rhythmic tune. Encourage them to move from one foot to the other to begin with, and then to use their arms to stretch and reach to each side.

Classroom review
Ask the children to recall and talk about some of the words they have used, using the flashcards as prompts if necessary.

Assessing learning outcomes
Do the children understand the words *stretch*, *stamp*, *stand*, *sit*, *slide* and *still*? Can they demonstrate the difference between a shiver and a shake?

The Wizard of Oz

In this series of lessons, selected aspects of the story *The Wizard of Oz* will be used as the stimulus for dance. Children will be encouraged to explore basic dance actions such as:

- travelling, jumping and turning
- using different parts of their bodies
- thinking about their own feelings and those of others
- creating, remembering and performing a series of action phrases
- using their imaginations to perform with increasing control and co-ordination.

They will be encouraged to select actions from those they have tried that are appropriate to the stimuli and the accompaniment , listening, responding and performing to the changes in the music and planning and developing phrases with rhythmic qualities. They will also have opportunities to work individually, with a partner and in a large class group and to copy, watch and describe dance movement.

There will be excellent opportunities to provide links with literacy. Through the course of the units, children will be introduced to descriptive vocabulary in the following areas:

- feelings – *cowardly, timid, afraid; strong, bold, brave*
- quality of movement – *strong/light, quick/slow, smooth/jerky*
- pathways
- body actions
- shapes the body can make
- parts of the body.

You may find it helpful to have pictures of the characters from the story displayed in the classroom and/or the hall as stimuli and reminders for the children.

UNIT: The Wizard of Oz

Enquiry questions	Learning objectives	Teaching activities	Learning outcomes
How do the cyclone and the Scarecrow move?	• Move individual body parts and practise a simple walking action in time with a beat, individually, then matching a partner. • Lead and follow with a partner. • Explore and develop turning, circling and spinning in different directions. • Select, practise and combine travelling, leaping and turning actions. • Explore and practise a variety of slow, floppy actions to imaginatively represent the Scarecrow. • Link together a phrase of actions.	Warm-up: clapping then walking in time with the beat; moving elbows up and down and hips from side to side, alternating these actions; developing a sequence of two then four actions; showing to, then matching with, a partner. Development: describing the action of a cyclone; practising swaying, circling, turning, spinning and whirling in different ways; developing the phrases of an action using different shapes and levels; practising running, jumping and turning in the air; choosing three of these actions to link together; practising stopping suddenly; practising floppy, disjointed actions and developing a phrase. Dance: linking together and practising parts of scarecrow sequence; practising cyclone phrases. Cool-down: walking slowly then swaying gently to relax.	Children: • portray the floppy actions of the Scarecrow • remember and respond to the accompaniment with their travelling and turning
How does the Tin Man move?	• Explore and practise stiff, jerky actions to imaginatively represent the Tin Man. • Imaginatively use different pathways to represent the journey along the yellow brick road. • Practise a walking action in time with a beat using different pathways. • Explore and develop a variety of turning actions at different levels and speeds.	Warm-up: clapping then walking to the rhythm of 'Follow the Yellow Brick Road'; using different pathways; practising a phrase then taking turns to lead and follow. Development: practising the sequence of three cyclone actions; trying slow, turning actions at different levels; practising a sequence of turns; practising stiff, jerky walking and running actions, movements of individual parts of the body, jumps and turning actions; developing a sequence of stiff, jerky movements. Dance: in pairs, taking turns to be the Tin Man while a partner oils the joints; practising cyclone actions. Cool-down: swaying gently to 'Somewhere Over the Rainbow'; walking slowly and relaxing.	• incorporate different levels into their ideas for the cyclone • move individual parts of the body • understand what is meant by *stiff* and *jerky*
How does the Cowardly Lion behave?	• Create a simple step pattern in time with an accompaniment. • Explore contrasting feelings using different movement actions. • Explore and practise prowling and pouncing to imaginatively represent the Lion. • Revise and practise the Tin Man or Scarecrow sequence.	Warm-up: walking lightly, practising stopping and starting and striding strongly using different pathways to 'Follow the Yellow Brick Road'. Development: using words like *prowl* and *pounce* and qualities like *strong* and *brave* to represent the Lion in posture, gesture and movement; developing a phrase of these actions; trying a pouncing action then joining some of these actions together; using words like *weak*, *cowardly* and *timid* and trying out cowering shapes, shaking and retreating actions. Dance: developing a phrase – shake, creep, hide; combining a phrase – strong and proud, retreat and creep backwards, hide and shake with fear; practising the Tin Man or Scarecrow sequence. Cool-down: stretching and clenching hands and then bodies; swaying gently.	• remember and repeat short phrases of movement • keep time with an accompaniment • use words and movement to demonstrate contrasting feelings
How do the witches move?	• Practise skipping individually and in pairs, in time with music. • Develop and practise a Good Witch and Wicked Witch dance in pairs. • Practise melting actions. • Explore dance actions using contrasting qualities to represent the good and bad witches.	Warm-up: walking lightly to 'We're Off to See the Wizard'; practising stopping and starting and skipping. Development: practising smooth, light continuous steps, turning actions, gestures and other actions using changes of level; practising twisted, jagged shapes, jerky steps and jumps; linking three jumps together. Dance: developing a sequence for the Wicked Witch and practising the Good Witch sequence; in pairs, practising the Good Witch and Wicked Witch dance with a melting action to finish. Cool-down: shaking arms then legs then whole bodies; stretching; practising slow, melting actions.	• understand and use contrasting actions • perform different actions for the Good and Wicked Witches

Enquiry questions	Learning objectives	Teaching activities	Learning outcomes
How can we find the way through the dark wood?	• Use movement imaginatively to follow the pathway through the dark wood. • Use the prepositions *under, over, around, through, along*. • Make a range of different shapes individually and in pairs. • Explore and try out sleepy, drowsy actions. • Revise, practise and refine aspects of a dance from a previous lesson.	Warm-up: moving to music; playing 'Statue shapes'. Development: practising different ways of creeping; selecting three ways to link together; practising making tall and low twisted shapes; in pairs, making twisted shapes together. Dance: pairs taking turns to make twisted shapes while others creep following each other around, under, over, or through the shapes; practising one of the dance sequences from past lessons. Cool-down: walking slowly and getting sleepier; stretching, yawning and curling.	• show imagination in actions and ideas for travelling through the dark wood • use different levels • demonstrate fear in their movements
Practise and perform aspects of *The Wizard of Oz*	• Practise and refine selected aspects of the story in dance. • Link together a series of actions. • Perform a dance in front of half the class. • Observe and comment on the performance of others.	Warm-up: practising step pattern to 'Follow the Yellow Brick Road'. Development: practising and refining linked actions from previous weeks. Dance: practising cyclone, scarecrow, lion, Tin Man, pathways and step pattern for 'Follow the Yellow Brick Road', the good and the Wicked Witch, the dark, scary forest; observing and commenting. Cool-down: walking slowly, getting sleepier and drooping, sinking and curling up; stretching and yawning.	• remember the qualities of the different actions and perform them well • remember the actions and qualities.

Cross-curricular links
English: telling, retelling, describing and sequencing a story; using words to describe the actions and emotions of characters.
Geography: learn about weather, winds and cyclones.
Science: looking at metals, changing states (for example rust).

Resources
A version of *The Wizard of Oz* by L Frank Baum (such as edited by Rosemary Border, Oxford Bookworms; edited by Susan Wolstenholme, Oxford World Classics); CD of *The Wizard of Oz – Original Motion Picture Soundtrack*; pictures of cyclones; pictures from the film of the Scarecrow, Tin Man, Lion and Good and Wicked Witches; tambour; tambourine; wood blocks; bells; cymbals.

The Wizard of Oz

(30 mins) How do the cyclone and the Scarecrow move?

What you need and preparation

You will need: the story *The Wizard of Oz*; a CD or tape of *The Wizard of Oz*, in particular, the songs 'Cyclone', 'If I Only Had a Brain' and 'Somewhere Over the Rainbow'; a tambourine; a tambour.

Read and discuss *The Wizard of Oz* in the classroom before this lesson, giving particular emphasis to the cyclone, what it is and the qualities of the actions. Remind the children of the rhyme 'Jingle jangle scarecrow'.

Display pictures of cyclones from books and magazines.

What to do

(7 mins) Warm-up

Ensure that the children are well spaced to start the warm-up. Ask them to clap in time with the beat of the tambour, and then to walk on the spot in the same time. Alternate these clapping and walking actions several times, encouraging the children to keep with the beat. (For example, clapping, walking, clapping, walking – eight beats or four beats.)

Ask the children to walk lightly in and out of spaces all over the hall to the beat of the tambour. Encourage good spacing. Emphasise light, brisk steps and use of different directions. Practise this, then encourage walking for eight beats in one direction and then eight beats in another.

Then tell the children to move their elbows up and down and then their hips from side to side in time with the same beat. Alternate these actions, encouraging the children to keep in time with the beat. Similarly, ask them to think of other parts of their body that they can move in time with the beat and practise those (for example head nod and shoulder shrug).

Help the children to choose and develop a sequence of two, then four actions. For example, tap knees, walk, shrug shoulders and move hips. (Use eight or four counts and then change.) Practise and see if the children can remember the sequence. Organise them into twos and ask them to take it in turns to show their partner this sequence. Encourage partners to join in and match the actions as soon as they are able to. Ensure that they take it in turns to lead.

(12 mins) Development

Ask the children if they can remember what a cyclone is. *In the story, what did it do to Dorothy's house? Can you describe the action?* (Turning, spinning, whirling.) *Can you try that action in movement?*

Ask them to sway gently from side to side (and later forwards and backwards), just moving their shoulders to begin with and then transferring their weight from one foot to the other on the spot. Encourage them to imagine that they are being blown gently by the wind. Gradually develop this into swaying, sweeping and circling as if they are being blown by a stronger wind. Prompt individual responses within the framework of the phrase (sway and sway and sway and circle).

Encourage them to think of and practise other ways they could make circles in the air (for example forwards and backwards) with their whole bodies. Try two or three ways in different directions. Let the children choose and practise their favourite ways of swaying and circling.

Ask them to try to spin around on the spot. Provide a short accompaniment (shaking tambourine) to give a framework for their actions (spin and spin and stop).

Encourage the children to think of and try different ways to turn or spin (long and thin; small and tucked; on one foot; on bottoms; using both feet), and particularly emphasise different levels. In order to avoid any children getting giddy, keep the phrase short and use both directions.

After listening to a fast beat and a bang of the tambourine (*tap, tap, tap, bang*), encourage the children to run and run and then jump into the air.

PRIMARY FOUNDATIONS: Physical education Ages 5–7

The Wizard of Oz

Vocabulary
cyclone
scarecrow
travelling
leaping
turning
spiralling

Ask the children to imagine themselves being blown about and tossed up in to the air by the wind and then try this several times. Watch for individual imaginative responses, particularly twists or turns in the air or expressive use of the arms, legs or whole body. Use one or two ideas as demonstrations and then encourage the children to try again; to practise and improve their actions. Briefly help them to practise their turning jumps as if they were being blown into the air by the cyclone.

Ask them to choose three of these actions to link together (for example run and leap, run and jump, run and turning jump), and to practise them with the accompaniment. Use percussion or 'Cyclone' from the soundtrack.

What might happen if the wind stopped suddenly? Encourage the children to finish their sequences by sinking quickly to the ground, suddenly but carefully. (Shake and bang the tambourine.) Get them to think of different shapes and positions for their collapsed shape as their finishing position.

Next, remind them about the Scarecrow in the story, who was stuffed with straw. Ask the children how they think he might walk and to show you some of their ideas to the accompaniment (a slow uneven beat – shake and tap the tambourine). Look for floppy, disjointed actions (see Diagram 3) and encourage these qualities.

Diagram 3

Ask the children if they remember the rhyme 'Jingle jangle scarecrow'. Encourage them to practise floppy movements with different parts of the body in turn (elbows, head, knees, shoulders) using a phrase of accompaniment (to words or shaking tambourine – *flop and flop and FLOP* – or 'If I Only Had a Brain' or the rhyme 'Jingle jangle scarecrow'). Together, develop this into a phrase to repeat and practise.

Ask the children to practise a floppy action on just one side of their body and then on the other. Then ask them to try out and practise a floppy jump and a floppy turning action using the same accompaniment.

8 mins Dance

Help the children to link these scarecrow movements together to create a slow scarecrow sequence. For example: flop, flop, flop (parts of the body); floppy step, step, step, step; floppy turn or jump; and floppy collapse of one side of the body to finish. Practise the sequence several times in time with the accompaniment (to *flop and flop and FLOP* or 'If I Only Had a Brain' or 'Jingle jangle scarecrow'). Encourage large, rhythmic, whole-body actions.

Ask the children to remember and practise linking their three travelling and turning actions to represent the cyclone that they tried earlier. (For example, run and leap; run and jump; run and turning jump.) Remind them to add their sudden, collapsed position to finish with (to words or the shaking tambourine or the song).

3 mins Cool-down

Encourage the children to walk slowly around the room, tall and upright (contrast this with their floppy movements) and then to stand in a space.

Ask them to sway gently from side to side. Start with a big side to side action, stepping and reaching to the sides, and then gradually reduce the size of the action until it is just a small movement of the shoulders. Encourage smooth, continuous movements. Use the first part of 'Somewhere Over the Rainbow' as far as *wish upon a star*. Ask everyone to relax to finish.

The Wizard of Oz

Classroom review

Ask the children to describe the actions of the cyclone and the Scarecrow to you or to a partner, and to say what they liked doing best and what they could do to improve this next time.

Assessing learning outcomes

How well did the children portray the floppy actions of the Scarecrow? Were they able to remember and respond to the accompaniment with their travelling and turning?

(30 mins) How does the Tin Man move?

Learning objectives
● Explore and practise stiff, jerky actions to imaginatively represent the Tin Man.
● Imaginatively use different pathways to represent the journey along the yellow brick road.
● Practise a walking action in time with a beat, using different pathways.
● Explore and develop a variety of turning actions at different levels and speeds.

Lesson organisation
Whole-class discussion; warm-up and performances individually and then in pairs; individual cool-down; teacher-led classroom review.

Vocabulary
cyclone
Tin Man
jerky
stiff
travelling
leaping
turning

What you need and preparation

You will need: the story and CD or cassette of *The Wizard of Oz*, in particular, 'Follow the Yellow Brick Road' and 'If I Only Had a Heart'; CD or tape player; a tambourine; a tambour; wood blocks.

Recap the story of *The Wizard of Oz* in the classroom before this lesson, giving particular emphasis to the winding pathway of the yellow brick road and talk about the scarecrow actions they tried in the last session. Have the children seen a scarecrow? *What do they do? What other characters are there in the story?* Discuss the Tin Man and how he might move. *What happens to metal if it is left out in all weathers?*

What to do

(5 mins) Warm-up
Ensure that the children are well spaced to start the warm-up. Ask them to listen to, then clap to, the rhythm of 'Follow the Yellow Brick Road'. Then ask them to walk around the room with a lively, light step, keeping time with the music. Encourage them to swing their arms easily at their sides as they do this.

Say that you want them to walk in straight lines, changing to move in another direction when they need to (encourage walking on the spot until there is space to move forward to help raise awareness of others).

Ask them to try a zigzag pathway, walking just a few steps and then turning sharply to walk in another straight line. For example, *Follow the yellow brick road* (walk in one direction), turn and *Follow the yellow brick road* (walk in another direction).

Next, ask them to try a smooth, continuous, curving, winding pathway as they walk.

Ask them to choose which pathway they will start with (curving or zigzag). Tell them to practise that first and then add a second pathway. Practise walking these interesting pathways one after the other. Some children may need help to discern when to change from one to the other.

In pairs, one behind the other (a step away), tell the children to take turns to lead and to follow. Encourage the leader to walk in an interesting pathway, with their partner following, listening to the beat and matching their step. Ensure that they take it in turns to lead.

(12 mins) Development
Discuss the fact that the cyclone in the story leads to the world of Oz and that is why we are using it to start the dance.

Ask the children to remember the three different actions they tried last time for the cyclone and to practise the sequence (run and leap; run and jump; run and turning jump) with the accompaniment.

Ask them to try a slow, turning action on the spot and then to turn in the other direction. Then ask them to turn as low as they can near the ground and then as high up as they can, stretching their arms up high. Practise a sequence with them, starting with a low turn and then travelling to a new space as if being swept along by the wind (turn and turn and travel and travel). In their new

space, ask them to try another turning action, this time rising up as they turn (travel, turn and rise). Tell everyone to repeat the sequence to the sound of the shaking tambourine.

Now ask the children to try a low starting position; turn and turn on the spot; travel to a new space; and then to turn and turn at the other level. Practise this phrase, encouraging them to link the movements together smoothly. Use 'Cyclone' or a shaking tambourine as an accompaniment.

Ask them to think of the Tin Man in the story, and to tell you how he might move (stiffly, jerkily). Play some short, sharp beats with the wood blocks.

Practise stiff, jerky walking and running actions, and stiff, jerky movements of individual parts of the body. Then practise jumping in a stiff, jerky way and stiff, jerky turning actions (see Diagram 4).

Ask the children to choose two or three of these ideas to include in a Tin Man sequence. Guide them by giving them a framework for their actions. A possible sequence could be:
- stiff, jerky movement of chosen body parts
- stiff, jerky running action
- stiff jumping action
- stiff movements of individual parts of the body.

Ask the children what happens if metal gets rusty. Ask them to show you how difficult it is to make some of the movements of the Tin Man, because their joints are very stiff and rusty.

Diagram 4

10 mins Dance

In pairs, ask the children to take it in turns to be the Tin Man (ensure fair turns). The Tin Man should hold a still, awkward shape. The Tin Man's partner picks up a huge oil can and one by one oils the joints. As each joint is oiled, that part begins to move until the whole body is moving. The Tin Man then walks or runs and then jumps or turns while the partner watches and claps. Ask the pairs to change over, and practise.

Remind them of some of their ideas for the cyclone and practise those to the music.

3 mins Cool-down

Ask the children to sway gently from side to side. Start with a big side to side action and then gradually reduce the size of the action until it is just a small movement of the shoulders. Encourage smooth, continuous movements. Use 'Somewhere Over the Rainbow' as the accompaniment. Then ask the children to shake down and relax.

Classroom review

Talk to the children, and encourage them to tell you about the Tin Man in the story. Discuss the ways they changed their movements when performing as a rusty Tin Man as compared with a well-oiled Tin Man.

Assessing learning outcomes

Are the children beginning to incorporate different levels into their ideas for the cyclone? Are they able to move individual parts of the body? Do they understand what is meant by *stiff* and *jerky*?

Follow-up activities
- Look at chemical changes which cause metals to change state.
- Perform experiments to test the effects of the air, water and salt water on iron.
- Look at other metals in water.
- Investigate how to stop metals rusting (paint, grease and so on).

The Wizard of Oz

(30 mins) How does the Cowardly Lion behave?

Learning objectives
- Create a simple step pattern in time with an accompaniment.
- Explore contrasting feelings using different movement actions.
- Explore and practise prowling and pouncing to imaginatively represent the Lion
- Revise and practise the Tin Man or scarecrow sequence.

Lesson organisation
Whole-class discussion; individual performances; teacher-led classroom review.

Vocabulary
strong
firm
brave
cowardly
timid
afraid
retreat
prowl
clench fist
pounce

What you need and preparation
You will need: a tape or CD player; the story and tape or CD of *The Wizard of Oz*, in particular, 'Follow the Yellow Brick Road' and 'Somewhere Over the Rainbow'; a tambourine; a tambour; cymbals.

Before the session, discuss with the children feelings of bravery and fear. If necessary, explain what is meant by being cowardly.

What to do

(7 mins) Warm-up
Ask the children to walk lightly on the spot to the tap of the tambourine. Practise stopping when the beat stops and starting when it plays again.

Ask the children to walk and then stride around the hall looking for all the spaces as the beat gets stronger. Check good spacing and encourage firm, brisk actions. Use demonstrations to show good use of space. Ask the children if they can remember and then try some of the pathways that they tried last time.

Ask them to stride or walk to the tune of 'Follow the Yellow Brick Road'. Then ask them if they can try out another step that they can do to this music (for example step, hop; skip; fancy walk), and to practise that several times. Encourage them to use the space well until their pulse is raised.

(10 mins) Development
Ask the children how a lion might move. Select action words from those suggested, such as *prowl* and *pounce*, and qualities like *strong* and *brave*. Ask the children to show you how they might stand if they were very strong, brave and proud. Look for examples of upright, strong, solid posture and help them to practise these. Practise a different position to each strong cymbal beat.

Tell the children to prowl around the hall with strong, brave strides or steps. Encourage a variety of responses (for example on two feet or on all fours) and use of different directions. There is no right or wrong way of interpreting and doing this, but emphasise the strong, brave qualities. Develop a phrase that incorporates prowling in one direction, prowling in another direction and then prowling and holding a strong, still shape. Encourage the children to include some extra actions of their own, for example large, clawing actions in the air or pawing the ground.

Ask the children to describe a pouncing action. Encourage them to use words (such as *quick jump, leap forwards or downwards, sudden swoop or attack*) and then to show you these in their movements. Practise this several times, providing a sudden, strong accompaniment (a–a–and… BANG, a–a–and… BANG), telling the children to get ready and then pounce, and again. Encourage them to join some of these actions together – starting with a strong starting position, then prowl, and prowl and prowl and proudly look around; prowl and prowl and pause and pounce and pounce and stand tall.

Ask the children what they think the opposite to being strong, brave and proud might be. Talk about the Lion in the story. *How did he feel?* Ask them for some descriptive words (*weak, cowardly, timid* and so on) and then to show you by their position that they are afraid. Look for good examples of weak, timid, cowering shapes.

What might the children do if they were very frightened? (Shake with fear and retreat.) *Try shaking and stopping in time with the shaking tambourine.* Ask them to creep around the hall with quiet, timid actions. Encourage lots of stopping and starting and hiding. Ask them to try moving backwards rather than going boldly forwards.

See how well the children can combine the shaking and the creeping as you play an accompaniment on the tambourine.

10 **Dance**
mins Encourage the children to develop the movements they have been practising into a phrase. (Shake and shake, creep and creep and creep and hide – introduce *cower* if it is appropriate, see Diagram 5 – creep and creep and hide.)

Diagram 5

Help the children to combine phrases, for example prowl strongly forward, proudly look around; retreat creeping backwards and hide; prowl strongly forward, proudly look around; retreat creeping backwards, hide and shake with fear. This could also be done in pairs.

Try to leave enough time to run through a brief revision and practise of the Tin Man or Scarecrow sequences.

3 **Cool-down**
mins Ask the children to stretch and clench their hands and then to stretch and curl their bodies. Finish with stretching and clenching fists.

Using 'Somewhere Over the Rainbow' as an accompaniment, ask the children to practise swaying and gently circling.

Classroom review

Ask the children to talk about how the Lion in the story felt and how he wanted to feel. Ask:
● What did you do to show that you were afraid? How did you move?
● What did you do to show that you were brave? How did you move?

Assessing learning outcomes

Can the children remember and repeat short phrases of movement? How well did their movements keep time with the accompaniment? Are they able to use words and movement to demonstrate contrasting feelings?

Follow-up activity
Discuss situations where children might be afraid, and how the mind can trick you at times like these.

The Wizard of Oz

(30 mins) How do the witches move?

Learning objectives
● Practise skipping, individually and in pairs, in time with music.
● Develop and practise a Good Witch and a Wicked Witch dance in pairs.
● Practise melting actions.
● Explore dance actions using contrasting qualities to represent the Good and Wicked Witches.

Lesson organisation
Whole-class discussion; individual and paired warm-up; dance individually and in pairs; individual cool-down; teacher-led classroom discussion.

Vocabulary
smooth
continuous
jagged
angular
exaggerate
casting spells

What you need and preparation

You will need: a tape or CD player; the story and soundtrack of *The Wizard of Oz*, in particular, 'We're Off to See the Wizard'; a tambourine; wood blocks; cymbals; Indian bells.

In the classroom, recap aspects of the story so far. Discuss the Good Witch and the Wicked Witch. *How would they move? What would the differences be?* Can the children think how they might show these in movement?

What to do

(5 mins) Warm-up
Start with everyone walking lightly on the spot to the tap of the tambourine and then to 'We're Off to See the Wizard'. Practise stopping when the beat stops and starting when it plays again.

Ask the children to try to skip around the room to the accompaniment. Encourage a regular rhythm with light steps. Encourage those who can skip easily to work with and help a partner, perhaps side by side or holding hands to feel the rhythm.

(12 mins) Development
Ask the children how they think the Good Witch might move. Listen to their responses and select ones that support and encourage smooth, calm, light and continuous qualities. Ask them to try some of their ideas to the accompaniment. Select some of the best ideas for everyone to develop.

Ask the children to practise slow, light, smooth steps to move forwards into a space. Observe responses and select demonstrations to emphasise gentle, continuous, smooth steps. Practise in time with the accompaniment and then encourage stepping in other directions.

Ask the children to try a smooth, calm and continuous turning action. Advise them to stretch out their arms and use their whole body in the action as they turn. Observe variations in response, and help children to develop or exaggerate parts of their action, emphasising the smooth, calm and continuous qualities. Look for and encourage changes of level (high, medium and low).

Remind the children of the classroom discussion about how the two witches might move, and the differences between the witches. Encourage them to think of what sorts of movement they could use to represent them.

Ask the children to imagine how the Good Witch would wave a wand in the air to cast spells. Suggest they start by reaching up high and help them to use all the space around them. Encourage smooth and continuous actions, moving from high to low positions and reaching out to the sides. Ask them to try some other actions (such as jumping, stirring and skipping) to represent the Good Witch. Encourage them to choose some or all of these ideas to incorporate into a sequence (for example, starting position, travelling action, turning action and casting a spell). Encourage them to listen to and practise with an accompaniment of slow, light taps with an Indian bell or cymbal.

Tell the children to show you a still, twisted shape to represent the Wicked Witch and then to try lots of others. Encourage them to make jagged, angular shapes. Ask them to link three of these shapes, as you beat the wood block, one after the other – *bang* (hold shape), *bang, bang*.

Ask the children to try a jerky stepping action to short sharp beats of the wood block. Again, encourage jerky, jagged, angular actions. Now ask them to imagine that they are waving their wand like the Wicked Witch (short, sharp, quick actions with bent knees and elbows). Similarly, ask them to try several twisted, jerky jumps to the short, strong beat and to choose three of these actions to link together.

11 mins **Dance**
Encourage the children to choose some of their Wicked Witch ideas to incorporate into a sequence. For example, jagged starting position, jump and jump and jump and travel, travel and cast a spell. Encourage them to listen to and practise with a wood-block accompaniment.

Ask them to remember their Good Witch sequence and to practise it to the sound of Indian bells.

Then tell everyone to find a partner and to number themselves 1 and 2. Number 1 will be the Wicked Witch first and number 2 the Good Witch. Ask them both to decide on their starting position and to hold it still. The Wicked Witch then dances around the Good Witch using the sequence practised earlier (jump and jump and jump and travel, travel and cast a spell), while the Good Witch stays still. The Wicked Witch then holds a still, jagged shape while the Good Witch dances around (travelling action, turning action and casting a spell). As the spell is cast, the Wicked Witch begins to melt. Encourage slow, melting actions to finish. Ensure that each child has the opportunity to perform both types of action.

2 mins **Cool-down**
Tell everyone to shake their arms, then their legs, then their whole bodies, and then to stretch up high. Repeat. Use a shaking tambourine as an accompaniment.

Lastly, ask everyone to practise the slow, melting actions from their high position, finishing in a low position lying on the ground. Use light taps of a cymbal or bell.

Classroom review
Ask the children to tell you about the differences between the movements of the two witches.

Assessing learning outcomes
Did the children understand, and could they use, the contrasting actions? Were there differences between the actions of the Good and Wicked Witches?

> **Follow-up activity**
> Write descriptively about the witches, what they look like and how they move.

---

30 mins # How can we find the way through the dark wood?

What you need and preparation
You will need: a tape or CD player; the story and CD or tape of *The Wizard of Oz*, in particular, 'We're Off to See the Wizard'; a tambourine; Indian bells.

Discuss what the characters felt as they made their way through the dark wood. Ask the children what they think it might be like to have to try to find their way through a dark wood or forest like the characters in the story. (Scary, frightening, worrying and so on).

What to do
5 mins **Warm-up**
Practise skipping and moving to 'We're Off to See the Wizard', using all the space.

Play a version of 'Musical statues', asking the children to make a shape to represent one of the characters when the music stops.

Ask them to show you these different shapes in turn – stretched wide, narrow, curled, twisted, fierce, proud, small, and so on.

12 mins **Development**
Remind the children how the characters felt as they tried to find their way through the dark wood. Ask: *How would you show these emotions through movement?*

> **Learning objectives**
> ● Use movement imaginatively to follow the pathway through the dark wood.
> ● Use the prepositions *under, over, around, through, along.*
> ● Make a range of different shapes, individually and in pairs.
> ● Explore and try out sleepy, drowsy actions.
> ● Refine aspects of a dance from a previous lesson.

The Wizard of Oz

Lesson organisation
Teacher-led discussion in the classroom; individual warm-up; individual and paired practice; dance routine in fours or as a class; individual cool-down; teacher-led classroom review.

Vocabulary
scary
frightening
afraid
fear
twisted
entwined

Ask the children to creep in and out of the space. Encourage light, quiet steps and use of different directions. Ask them if they can think of other ways of creeping and to try these. Use some of the children's ideas or help them to explore and practise some of these different ways of creeping:

- Creep along, keeping as low as you can to go under branches.
- Creep along as if balancing on a large trunk of a tree.
- Creep along as if squeezing through a narrow gap.
- Creep along as if trying not to tread in swampy areas.

Ask the children to select three of these ways, and to link them together into a phrase. What might be in their way as they make their way through the dark wood?

Now ask the children to make some tall, twisted shapes. Give them a shaking tambourine accompaniment to find the shape and to hold it still on the tap. Repeat this together, with several different shapes (move and hold, move and hold). Then do the same for some very *low*, twisted shapes.

In pairs, ask the children to make some tall, twisted shapes together. Encourage them to think about and choose different levels and to decide together how they will link their bodies. As before, accompany them with a shaking tambourine to find the shape to hold it still on the tap. Repeat this exercise with several different shapes (move and hold, move and hold). Then ask the pairs to make a twisted shape like an archway or a shape with a large hole in it.

8 mins — Dance

Ask each pair to join another pair and to take it in turns to show their twisted shapes. Give them the tambourine accompaniment to support these actions. When they have done this, ask one pair to go first to make their shapes, while the others decide on a pathway, with one following the other (for example to creep around, under, over or through the shapes as appropriate). Give the groups time to practise and then ask them to change over. This could also be practised with half the class making shapes while the other half moves between the shapes.

Select one or more of the dance sequences covered in the previous lessons to practise and refine (for example the cyclone or the Lion).

5 mins — Cool-down
Ask the children to remember what happened when the characters in the story went through the poppy field. Ask them what sorts of actions they could use to show that they are getting very tired.

Tell everyone to walk slowly around the hall, using all the space. Ask the children to imagine that they are getting sleepier and sleepier and to make their steps get slower and slower while their bodies start to droop. Accompany them with slow, light taps on Indian bells.

Ask them to really stretch their bodies out as if they were yawning and stretching from tiredness, and then to curl up. Let everyone practise this several times to finish.

Classroom review

Ask the children what they saw in their imagination when they thought of the dark wood. How well do they think they translated this into movement?

Assessing learning outcomes

Did the children put a lot of imagination and thought into their actions and ideas for travelling through the dark wood? Did they use different levels? Could they demonstrate in their movements that they were afraid?

Follow-up activity
Continue a discussion about being afraid. *What do you do if you are lost?*

 Practise and perform selected aspects of *The Wizard of Oz*

What you need and preparation
You will need: a tape or CD player; the story and CD or tape of *The Wizard of Oz*; a tambourine; a tambour; wood blocks.

In the classroom, discuss the story and the dances performed over the previous weeks.

What to do

Warm-up
5 mins Encourage the children to revise and practise the step pattern to the accompaniment of 'Follow the Yellow Brick Road'.

Development
18 mins Ask the children to remember, practise and refine the following linked actions. In turn:
1. the cyclone
2. the Scarecrow
3. the Lion
4. the Tin Man
5. pathways and step pattern for 'Follow the Yellow Brick Road'
6. the Good and Wicked Witches
7. the dark and scary forest
8. the poppy field.

Dance
12 mins Briefly practise together the list in the Development section above.

Ask half the class to perform their sequences, while the other half observe and then comment on what they liked best and why. Change over so that everyone has a chance to show their ideas.

Ask them all to try it through once more. Acknowledge and thank the children for their efforts.

Cool-down
5 mins Ask the children to walk slowly around the hall using all the space. Ask them to show you that they are getting sleepier and sleepier (their steps should get slower and slower) and that parts of the body start to droop. Start with head, then shoulders, then one side, then the other. Encourage them to sink slowly to their knees and then to curl up.

While they are lying down, ask them to really stretch their bodies out as if they were yawning and then to curl up. Practise this several times to finish.

Classroom review
Ask the children to think back over previous lessons. *Which part of the story did you like doing best in dance and why?*

Assessing learning outcomes
Could the children remember the qualities of the different actions? Which did they do well? Which did they have difficulty with? Could they remember the actions and qualities?

Learning objectives
● Practise and refine selected aspects of the story in dance.
● Link together a series of actions.
● Perform a dance in front of half the class.
● Observe and comment on the performance of others.

Lesson organisation
Teacher-led recap in the classroom; individual warm-up; individual and paired practice; half-class performances; individual cool-down; teacher-led classroom discussion.

Follow-up activities
● Other possibilities for lessons include explorations in dance of the Munchkins, the Emerald City, throne room, Winged Monkeys, the discovery of Oz (the Wizard is a little old man working machines).
● Children could be encouraged to write about one of the characters in the story.
● Ask the children to draw their favourite character from the story.

Under the sea

This series of lessons will help children to experience and develop dance actions using the theme 'under the sea or waves'. A variety of travelling, jumping, turning, gesturing and stopping actions relevant to the topic will be explored and developed, emphasising appropriate qualities, such as fast and slow, strong and light, smooth and jerky.

Using poetry as a starting point in the classroom, children can be involved in selecting the key stimuli and then the key action words and qualities, and can discuss them in preparation for their dance. All the poems used are provided as photocopiable sheets – 'The Song of the Waves' by Bernard Martin, 'Fish' by Mary Ann Hoberman, 'The Eel' by Robert Oliver, 'Sea Snake' by Cora Rumble, and 'Under the Sea' by Christine Tubbage.

The lesson plans provide excellent opportunities for links with literacy, geography, science and art and design.

Children can be encouraged to appreciate and scrutinise the poetry, and even to write some of their own poems on a similar theme. They will learn about myths and legends of the sea, which could be used as a basis for their descriptive writing.

In terms of geography, children can be encouraged to investigate ocean environments, the creatures that live in them and the effects of over-fishing and pollution on marine wildlife.

The poems could lead on to links with the science curriculum, in particular the classification of species of sea creatures, the forces involved in floating and sinking, and the movement of waves caused by wind and the gravitational pull of the moon.

Children can also be encouraged to imagine, draw and paint the sea and sea creatures, storms and calm in their art and design lessons.

UNIT: Under the sea

Enquiry questions	Learning objectives	Teaching activities	Learning outcomes
How do waves move on calm and stormy seas?	● Practise ways of travelling forwards and backwards. ● Work in unison. ● Emphasise size and different levels. ● Combine a series of actions into a sequence to represent waves.	Warm-up: rubbing, shaking different parts of the body in time with the accompaniment; shaking feet and hands; pitter-pattering feet using curving pathways; turning and jumping. Development: practising forwards and backwards pitter-patter action to represent the waves, varying level and size of the action; matching this action with a partner; practising different tossing and turning jumps; practising splashing (light, quick movements) and turning and rolling near the ground. Dance: create a dance in pairs, linking phrases of the wave actions, starting gently, getting bigger, tossing and turning, finishing gently. Cool-down: rocking from side to side, stretching and wiggling fingers.	Children: ● are aware of each other in the space ● keep in time with their partners ● respond to the phrases of the accompaniment and link their actions
Can we improve our representations of waves?	● Explore actions of rising and sinking and travelling. ● Practise ways of travelling forwards and backwards. ● Work in pairs and then fours (in unison). ● Emphasise size. ● Combine a series of actions into a sequence to represent waves.	Warm-up: rubbing and shaking different parts of the body high and low, rising and sinking; tiptoe rising and sinking. Development: practising a rippling action in arms then through the whole body; practising low, slow travelling actions forwards and backwards and sideways, rolling, spreading and reaching smoothly and gently. Dance: creating and practising a forwards and backwards sequence in pairs; practising phrases of action for the stormy sea, combining and reviewing. Cool-down: practising creeping and playing 'Shipwreck statues'; practising rippling action and relaxing.	● use appropriate vocabulary to describe calm and stormy seas ● are aware of individual parts of the body
How do small fish move?	● Practise quick, light travelling actions using smooth, swerving, curving and darting, angular, zigzag pathways. ● Explore wiggling parts of and the whole body. ● Practise running, leaping and turning in time with an accompaniment. ● Choose starting and finishing positions. ● Practise dancing in pairs, leading and following, using smooth curving, short darting and zigzag pathways. ● Combine a series of actions into a sequence to represent small fish.	Warm-up: practising wiggling parts and the whole body; practising tiptoeing, weaving in and out using curving pathways. Development: practising hurrying and scurrying, tiptoeing with curving pathways; in pairs, taking turns leading and following; developing phrases of scurrying and pausing; practising short, straight pathways darting to and fro, pausing and wiggling; practising flying with 'a leap and a bound'. Dance: practising leading and following; developing a dance sequence using curving and zigzag pathways; adding wiggling to the movement; practising leaping and turning jumps. Cool-down: swaying, reaching and circling.	● distinguish between curving and zigzag pathways ● lead and follow

UNIT: Under the sea

Enquiry questions	Learning objectives	Teaching activities	Learning outcomes
How do crabs move?	• Practise stopping and making different shapes. • Learn the words *scurry* and *scuttle* and practise them, moving sideways at different speeds. • Practise opening and closing at different speeds.	Warm-up: tiptoeing in and out of all the space, stopping and starting making statues (eel and starfish shapes). Development: practising different ways of moving sideways; practising scuttling and stopping suddenly and linking together to make a pattern; practising opening and closing, slowly and quickly; exploring and practising twisting and lowering. Dance: practising, linking and commenting constructively. Cool-down: stretching open slowly and closing, varying the speed of the action.	• perform the scuttling actions sideways in time with the accompaniment • understand *opening* and *closing* • use different speeds in their actions
How do eels and sea snakes move?	• Practise travelling in different directions, pathways and levels. • Practise curving, smooth, light actions of the body. • Explore and practise making strong shipwreck shapes in threes. • Remember a sequence of actions and respond appropriately to an accompaniment.	Warm-up: playing the starfish statues game, tiptoeing and making other shapes. Development: practising stretching, making long, thin shapes then twisting and coiling; practising wriggling and squirming smoothly and continuously, rising and sinking; practising light little steps making curving pathways; practising making strong, jagged shipwreck shapes in threes. Dance: practising crab then eel movements; creating and practising dance in threes, making strong shipwreck shapes, eel like movements and crab like movements in turn. Cool-down: swaying and waving arms smoothly all around.	• remember the sequence of actions • respond appropriately to the accompaniment
Can we create and perform an under-the-sea dance?	• Remember, repeat and link actions from the last few weeks. • Demonstrate awareness of the different qualities of the actions. • Respond appropriately to different forms of accompaniment and use different pathways.	Warm-up: playing the starfish statues game. Development: practising stretching and reaching smoothly and opening and closing like an anemone. Dance: choosing parts of the dances from the last few weeks to put together in a sequence, practise and refine. Cool-down: shaking arms, legs, then whole body; stretching slowly and then curling up small.	• remember the actions from the last few weeks • demonstrate an awareness of different qualities • respond to different forms of accompaniment.

Cross-curricular links
English: listening to poetry; understanding and using adverbs.
Geography and science: learning about the sea and sea creatures, the movement of waves.

Resources
Photocopiable pages 148–52; tape or CD player; *Carnival of the Animals* by Saint-Saëns; *Nutcracker Suite* by Tchaikovsky; a sound effects tape with the sound of waves; tambourine; wood blocks; cymbals; a long piece of ribbon; video recording and viewing equipment (optional).

(30 mins) How do waves move on calm and stormy seas?

What you need and preparation

Read through the poem on photocopiable page 148 as a class before going to the hall, and encourage discussion about the action words that describe wave movement and a stormy sea: *tossing*, *rolling*, *turning* and *splashing*.

You will need: a tape or CD player; sound effects of waves; a tambourine; a long, large ribbon or piece of material to simulate the action of a wave.

What to do

(5 mins) Warm-up

Ask the children to sit in a space and rub their elbows, then their feet. Play *tap, tap, tap, pause* on the tambourine as an accompaniment and ask the children to alternate from one part of the body to another. Change to shaking those parts in turn, accompanied by shaking the tambourine in phrases.

Ask the children to tap their feet on the floor slowly, quickly, slowly, quickly in response to the tambourine as it changes speed. Repeat with the hands tapping, then alternate (feet, hands, feet, hands).

Now tell everyone to stand in a space and to pitter-patter their feet on the spot (lots of light, little steps). Experiment with this, gradually getting faster and then slower in time with the accompaniment (shaking tambourine).

Encourage the children to pitter-patter their feet as they move around the hall. Check their spacing and encourage them to use curving pathways as they use all the space. Emphasise light, quick, small steps.

Ask them to try to turn and jump when they hear the louder taps on the tambourine as they move about the hall. Practise this several times.

(12 mins) Development

Explain to the children that they will be trying to represent the movement of waves, as in the poem you read in class. Ask them to face you in a space and to pitter-patter their feet as they move a few steps towards you and then a few steps backwards away from you. Check their spacing, and encourage them to do this as a group rather than with individual timing, giving them a clear indication of the phrasing (pitter-patter towards… pitter-patter back, and so on).

Ask the children to think about how they could include their arms to emphasise the forwards and backwards movement, and encourage them to try their ideas to the same pitter-patter phrase (see Diagram 6). Practise this and then, prompting with the long ribbon, select a few individuals to demonstrate a sweeping flowing action in which their arms go forwards and backwards (or other interesting and appropriate ideas).

Diagram 6

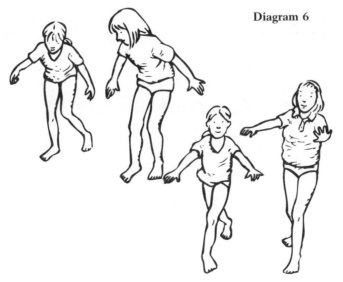

Learning objectives
● Practise ways of travelling forwards and backwards.
● Work in unison.
● Emphasise size and different levels.
● Combine a series of actions into a sequence to represent waves.

Lesson organisation
Whole-class discussion; individual and group performances; then in pairs and fours; individual cool-down; teacher-led classroom review.

Vocabulary
waves
advancing
retreating
stormy
tossing
rolling
turning
splashing
rising
sinking
calm
flowing gently
rippling
lapping
creeping
spreading

Practise this and, once they have grasped the phrasing, the children could add gentle *ssssshhhhhhh* sounds like the waves.

Ask the children to work with a partner, starting side by side, and to try moving (pitter-patter feet) forwards and backwards, keeping in time with each other and the accompaniment.

Ask them to try to include a change of level in their movements (for example higher to begin with and then lower as they come forwards). Encourage them to repeat the phrase (forwards and backwards) starting small and gradually making their movement bigger.

Remind the children of the discussion about some of the action words that describe a stormy sea: *tossing*, *rolling* and *turning*. Starting with *tossing* and *turning*, ask them to practise turning jumps, first of all one way and then the other.

Encourage them to try 'tossing' in different ways – at different levels, with different shapes, with different parts of their body held high (for example hands, knees or elbows). Look for imaginative and unusual responses and encourage them to practise two or three of their favourites.

Now ask them to think about splashing and how they could use light, quick movements of the hands, elbows or feet to stretch out into the space. Can they do splashing jumps in the air? Can they try to include some splashing actions as they move forwards and backwards like the waves?

Ask the children to think about, and try, turning when they are very near to the ground. This could be in a crouched position or like a sideways roll. Encourage them to try a few different ways and then to choose one special one to practise in time with the accompaniment.

10 mins Dance
In twos or fours:
● Ask the children to make up a short sequence, moving forwards and backwards like the waves. (If in fours, they could move in a line or two could start the forwards action reaching forwards and as they start to slowly move backwards keeping low, the second pair start their forwards action.
● Using the accompaniment (tambourine or sound effects) to help phrase the actions, encourage the children to start gently and lightly, keeping their actions small and then gradually making them bigger and bigger until they are jumping and travelling forwards and pitter-pattering their feet backwards. The phrase would be (each section twice): pitter-patter forward and back; larger pitter-patter and splashing; tossing and turning jumps and pitter-patter back; pitter-patter forward and back. Encourage the children to practise this several times, thinking about how they might refine their actions (for example keeping in time with the accompaniment and with each other or varying the size of the actions).

3 mins Cool-down

Ask the children to stand in a space and to rock from one foot to the other (side to side). Encourage them to transfer their weight smoothly, using their arms to reach and stretch to the side as they do this.

Ask them to stretch their arms up high above their heads and to wiggle their fingers, then to slowly and smoothly put their arms by their sides.

Classroom review
Ask the children to talk about the movement of the waves and how they portrayed this in action. Emphasise the directions and the levels. How did they feel when they were trying the tossing and turning actions for the stormy sea?

Assessing learning outcomes
Are the children aware of each other in the space? Can they keep in time with their partners? Can they respond to the phrases of the accompaniment and link their actions?

Follow-up activities
● Ask the children to write descriptively (either prose or poetry) about the actions of a calm and a stormy sea.
● Invite the children to draw or paint representations of calm and stormy seas and the actions of the waves.

(30 mins) Can we improve our representations of waves?

What you need and preparation

Re-read through the poem on photocopiable page 148 as a class before going to the hall, and discuss last lesson's movement of the waves. Select and talk about key words for stormy and calm seas.

You will need: a tape or CD player; sound effects of waves; a tambourine; bells; a long, large ribbon or piece of material to simulate the action of a wave.

What to do

(5 mins) Warm-up

Ask the children to sit in a space and to rub their shoulders, then their ankles. Shake the tambourine as an accompaniment, and ask the children to alternate from one part of the body to another. Change to shaking those parts in turn.

Ask the children to shake one foot, then the other foot, then both feet in the air (shake and shake and shake and stop), quickly in response to the same sound. Then repeat with the hands shaking.

Tell them to choose part of themselves to shake and to shake that part high and then low. Emphasise rising and sinking as they shake. Ask them to choose a low or a high starting position for this (shake and shake and change level; shake and shake and change level).

Now ask them to tiptoe around the hall using all the spaces. Check their spacing, encourage different directions and then ask them to try rising and sinking as they travel.

(8 mins) Development

Ask the children to try a gentle rippling action in their arms. Try one arm first, then the other, then both together. Then encourage them to think about, and try, a gentle rippling action right through their bodies. Demonstrate the rippling action by using the long ribbon and then practise it in phrases (ripple, ripple and pause; ripple, ripple and pause) using a part then the whole body, and again.

Ask the children to think of some words for a very calm sea: *flowing gently, rippling, lapping, creeping, spreading*. Playing a very slow, gentle accompaniment (or sound effects of the sea), ask the children to move gently and smoothly, flowing forwards and backwards. Encourage them to keep low and slow. Draw their attention to the contrast with the tossing and jumping for the stormy sea.

Starting from a low position (on bottom, knees or tummy), encourage the children to try reaching out, spreading in different directions (in front, behind, to the sides). Encourage them to use different parts of the body to do this (for example hands, feet, elbows) smoothly and gently. Use the sound of gentle lapping of waves, vocal sounds or continuous sound of light bells to accompany this.

Encourage the children to keep low and to roll sideways and spread slowly out as they move forwards. Practise this and then add the pitter-patter travelling action when gently back on their feet. Develop these into a phrase that is repeated: forwards and spread and gently back; forwards and spread and gently back.

(13 mins) Dance

Repeat and practise moving gently and smoothly, flowing forwards and backwards in pairs or fours. Then ask the children to add a movement keeping low and rolling sideways, spreading slowly out as they move forwards. Practise this and then develop the pitter-patter travelling action as they get gently back to their feet.

Learning objectives
● Explore actions of rising and sinking and travelling.
● Practise ways of travelling forwards and backwards.
● Work in pairs and then fours (in unison).
● Emphasise size.
● Combine a series of actions into a sequence to represent waves.

Lesson organisation
Whole-class discussion; individual warm-up; individual, paired and small-group performances; cool-down individually and in threes; teacher-led classroom review.

Vocabulary
waves
advancing
retreating
stormy
tossing
rolling
turning
splashing
rising
sinking
calm
flowing gently
rippling
lapping
creeping
spreading

When the children have worked out their sequence and formation, ask them to listen to the accompaniment that gets stronger and quicker from the previous session (see page 40), gradually adding the phrases of action for the stormy sea. Highlight the contrasts in movement quality from light to strong and slow to quick. Practise and review.

(4 mins) Cool-down
Ask the children to creep slowly around the room to the sound of light bells and explain that when you say *Stop* or *Shipwreck*, they are to get into threes to make a strong, jagged shape.

Ask them to practise, on their own in a space, the rippling action through their bodies. Relax.

Classroom review
Ask the children to describe their actions for the calm sea and then the stormy sea.

Assessing learning outcomes
Can the children use appropriate vocabulary to describe calm and stormy seas? Are they aware of individual parts of the body?

(30 mins) How do small fish move?

Learning objectives
● Practise quick, light travelling actions using smooth, swerving, curving and darting, angular, zigzag pathways.
● Explore wiggling parts of and the whole body.
● Practise running, leaping and turning in time with the accompaniment.
● Choose starting and finishing positions.
● Practise dancing in pairs, leading and following, using smooth curving, short darting and zigzag pathways.
● Combine a series of actions into a sequence to represent small fish.

What you need and preparation
Read through the poem on photocopiable page 149 as a class before going to the hall, and pick out and discuss key actions words about the movement of small fish.

You will need: a CD or tape player; 'Aquarium' from *Carnival of the Animals* by Saint-Saëns; a tambourine.

What to do
(5 mins) Warm-up
Ask the children to wiggle their bodies (wiggle and stop, wiggle and stop) to a shaking tambourine. Ask them if they can try wiggling just their shoulders, just their hips, just their knees, just their elbows. Ask them to describe this action and then to try it again. Encourage small, light shaking actions. Encourage them to try this as they move up and down on the spot.

Then ask them to tiptoe around the hall as lightly as they can, weaving in and out of each other, always looking for spaces. Encourage them to make curving pathways, swerving smoothly to stay in a space. Choose two or three children to demonstrate light feet, good use of space and smooth travelling actions.

(10 mins) Development
Introduce two words from the fish poem – *hurrying* and *scurrying*. Ask the children to find a partner and to number themselves 1 and 2. Number 1 is the leader and 2 follows their smooth swerving, curving pathways as they hurry and scurry in and out all over the space. Change over so that number 2 has a chance to lead and number 1 can follow. Give the children a clear framework for these travelling actions by providing phrases of sound with a pause (on the tambourine: *shake, shake, shake, shake, shake, shake, shake and pause*, and repeat). Emphasise smooth, continuous curving pathways and very light footwork.

This time, ask the children to try short, straight pathways to a slightly faster accompaniment with shorter phrases (*shake and shake and stop, shake and shake and stop*). Emphasise the sharp change of direction as they make zigzag pathways and dart this way and that. Encourage them to be sensitive to each other's movements, looking where they are going.

Ask them to add a wiggle on the stop before they move off into a new direction (shake and shake and wiggle).

In a space on their own again, ask everyone to run and leap into the air – *Fly with a leap and a bound*. If they can, ask them to jump and turn (whisking). Practise light landings, one foot after the other, trying to smoothly continue running. Stress that they do this lightly and as quietly as they can, *no one making the tiniest sound*.

(12 mins) Dance

In pairs, ask the children to choose curving, swerving pathways, then darting zigzag pathways and to practise them in time with the accompaniment (tambourine or 'Aquarium' from *Carnival of the Animals*) with one leading and one following. Make sure they take it in turns to practise leading and following. Choose two pairs to demonstrate the different pathways and then encourage them all to think of ways they can improve their sequences (for example clear pathways, good use of space, light footwork). Ask everyone to try again to make theirs better.

Ask the pairs to think of a starting position for this sequence (such as both crouching low or one of them high and one low). Ask them to start wiggling one part of their body, then a bit more and then the whole body, and then to practise their light travelling actions with curving, then zigzag pathways.

Remind the class of the leaping and bounding actions they tried earlier and to choose turning jumps. Let them practise these individually and then incorporate them into the sequence – one partner leading curving pathways, then leaping and bounding individually away from their partner, and then back together again with the other partner following with zigzag pathways. Help them to use their imaginations with this part. Give them a clear indication when to change actions – wiggling, travelling in pairs, leaping individually, travelling – and when to change leaders.

(3 mins) Cool-down

Individually in a space, ask the children to sway from one foot to the other smoothly with their arms reaching from side to side. Finish by telling them to make a big circle above their heads with their arms.

Classroom review

Read the poem again and ask the children about some of the words they used in their dance. What were the different pathways that they tried?

Assessing learning outcomes

Can the children distinguish between curving and zigzag pathways? Are they able to lead and to follow in their pairs?

Lesson organisation
Discussion in the classroom; individual warm-up and practice; paired performances; individual cool-down; teacher-led classroom review.

Vocabulary
wiggle
swerve
scurry
whisk
dart
slide
glide
leap
bound

Follow-up activities
● Ask the children to find, read and discuss other poems about fish, and maybe even write one of their own.
● The children could be asked to draw or paint representations of fish.

(30 mins) How do crabs move?

Learning objectives
● Practise stopping and making different shapes.
● Learn the words *scurry* and *scuttle* and practise them, moving sideways at different speeds.
● Practise opening and closing at different speeds.

Lesson organisation
Classroom discussion; individual warm-up and practice; individual and paired performances; individual cool-down; teacher-led classroom review.

Vocabulary
crabs
scurry
scuttle
hide
bury
pincers
opening
closing
sideways

What you need and preparation

Read through the poem on photocopiable page 150 as a class before going to the hall, and enter into a whole-class discussion about the movement of creatures that live under the sea, particularly crabs. Discuss key action words for crabs – *scuttle*, *hide* and *bury*.

You will need: a CD or tape player; 'Aquarium' from *Carnival of the Animals* by Saint-Saëns; a tambourine; wood blocks.

What to do

(5 mins) Warm-up

Start by asking the children to tiptoe on the spot and then around the hall, moving forwards and sideways, stopping and starting in time with the accompaniment (shaking tambourine or 'Aquarium' from *Carnival of the Animals*) like 'Musical statues'. Then introduce to them a game in which, when you say *Eel* they stop in a long, thin shape, and when you say *Starfish* they make a starfish shape. Practise this, using the curving pathways of the fish when you say *Fish*.

(10 mins) Development

Ask the children to practise stepping sideways. Start slowly and encourage them to try sideways steps *without* crossing their feet and then sideways steps *with* crossing their feet.

Develop this into a sideways scuttling action by gradually increasing the speed. Encourage the children to use only a few steps before pausing and moving sideways in the other direction (scuttle, scuttle, scuttle, pause). Check their use of space.

Ask the children to think of, and then try, other ways they can move sideways (such as on all fours, on hands and knees, on their tummies). Ask them to think of crabs scuttling sideways and to try that in their movement. Look for and encourage a variety of responses, emphasising the quick movement sideways. Gradually speed this up, although this might be more difficult on some parts. Emphasise the scuttling, sideways movement rather than just trying to 'be' crabs.

Try out scuttling and then stopping suddenly (scuttle, scuttle, scuttle, stop) to represent the crab being still like a stone. Ask the children to try more than one way and then to choose one that they could practise in time with the accompaniment (scuttle, scuttle one way and stop, scuttle, scuttle another way and stop).

Then ask them to scuttle and to practise stopping suddenly. Practise closing themselves up quickly or dropping down to the ground like a stone. Encourage sudden stillness, then suggest they rise up slowly, ready to scuttle again. Practise and refine these phrases in time with the accompaniment (shaking tambourine) – scuttle, scuttle one way and close/lower and stop, rise up slowly then scuttle, scuttle another way and stop.

Discuss with the children the pincer movement of a crab's claws. Ask the children to stretch their arms out wide and then to close them (open, close; open, close…). Encourage them to do this slowly and deliberately, stretching right through to their fingers and then squeezing their arms slowly and strongly together.

Ask them to stretch out slowly and then to suddenly 'snap' their arms closed again. Exaggerate the change of speed. Then ask the children to open and close their arms in another space. Can they think of other places (at the side of them, above their heads, behind their backs, low down)? Ask them to choose three different ways and to do them one after the other in time with the accompaniment (a quick beat on the wood block or sharp tap on the tambourine for the 'snap' action). Give them the phrase: open and close and change position, open and close and change position, open and snap shut.

Now ask the children to see if they can use any other parts of the body to open and close (for example legs, elbows or knees). Practise this, and select a few demonstrations to show original ideas or good quality of movement (in time, good stretch and close).

Talk to the children about the crabs burying themselves in the sand and see if they can try some ideas (such as twisting the body backwards and forwards on the spot, getting lower and lower) to the shaking tambourine. Practise rising up and sinking down.

10 mins Dance
Practise the scuttling actions in three phrases, starting slowly, getting quicker and then finishing with a sudden stop. Then add the burrowing movements. Develop these into a sequence by linking all the actions.

Ask the children to practise and refine the sequence and then in pairs to take it in turns to watch each other and to say what they liked about their crab-like movements. Encourage them to repeat their own sequence of actions.

5 mins Cool-down
Ask the children to tiptoe lightly in and out around the hall.

Ask them to stretch open slowly and to close slowly. Try this in standing and lying positions, then vary the speed of the action (open slowly, close quickly; open quickly, close slowly). Finish by opening slowly and closing slowly.

Classroom review

Back in the classroom, ask the children which actions are typical of a crab. *What were the special words used today?* (For example, *scuttling*.) What did the children like best about their performances?

Assessing learning outcomes

Could the children perform the scuttling actions sideways in time with the accompaniment? Did they understand *opening* and *closing*? Could they use different speeds in their actions?

30 mins How do eels and sea snakes move?

What you need and preparation

Read through photocopiable pages 151 and 152 as a class before going to the hall, and discuss the movement of eels and sea snakes. Discuss the key action words for this lesson – *stretch, squirm, slither, twist* and *coil*.

You will need: a CD or tape player; 'Aquarium' from *Carnival of the Animals* by Saint-Saëns; a tambourine; cymbals.

What to do

5 mins Warm-up
Ask the children to tiptoe in and out around the space. Remind them how to play the starfish statues game. Practise this before introducing some more shapes:
● Eel and sea snake – long, thin shape.
● Starfish – star shape.
● Crab – in pairs, back to back, hold each other's hands between legs.
● Octopus – in pairs with eight waving limbs.
● Shipwreck – in threes, make a sharp, jagged shape.

Learning objectives
● Practise travelling in different directions, pathways and levels.
● Practise curving, smooth, light actions of the body.
● Explore and practise making strong shipwreck shapes in threes.
● Remember a sequence of actions and respond appropriately to an accompaniment.

Under the sea

Lesson organisation
Classroom discussion; individual warm-up; individual, group and whole-class practice; individual cool-down; teacher-led classroom review.

Vocabulary
stretch
squirm
slither
twist
coil
shipwreck

10 mins Development
Ask the children to stretch out, making themselves as long and as thin as they can. Encourage this in different positions (lying, standing, on hands and feet). Play a cymbal and encourage them to keep stretching as long as they can hear the sound.

Encourage them to twist and coil their bodies in different ways and to practise this in time with the accompaniment (little taps on the cymbal).

Ask them to join the stretching and coiling together (to a long, continuous sound of the cymbal and then lots of little taps to coil up).

Now ask the children to try to wriggle through their bodies (with a shaking tambourine). Encourage them to bend and stretch and 'squirm'. Ask them to do this as smoothly and continuously as they can, and encourage rising and sinking as they do this.

Ask them to move around the hall with lots of light, little steps, winding in and out, making curving pathways, and then to try to add the flowing, stretching arm movements.

Ask the children to get into threes and to practise making strong, jagged shapes like a shipwreck. Bang on the tambourine for one shape and hold position, bang on the tambourine again for a second shape and hold position, bang on the tambourine for a third shape and hold position.

12 mins Dance
Ask the children to practise and refine their crab movements from the previous session, then practise the slinky, eel-like movement. Emphasise *slippery* and *sliding*.

Ask some of the children to show their strong shipwreck shapes in threes. Check their spacing. Ask some others to choose eel-like movements and the rest to choose sideways scuttling, hiding and burying crab-like movements. Ask them to listen to the accompaniment and then to choose a starting position:
- shipwreck shape (strong beat, hold the shape)
- long, thin eel shape (flowing action, weaving in and out of the shapes)
- closed crab shape (crab-like actions, scuttle, scuttle and stop, scuttle, scuttle and stop).

Try these again, asking the children to choose a different action.

3 mins Cool-down
Ask the children to stand in a space and to sway their arms from side to side above their heads. Ask them to wave their arms in front of them, to the side of them, behind them and above their heads again. Emphasise smoothly flowing actions.

Classroom review
Ask the children to discuss as a class the movements of the eel, the sea snake and the crab. *What words could you use to describe the eel, the sea snake and the crab?*

Assessing learning outcomes
Are the children able to remember the sequence of actions and respond appropriately to the accompaniment?

(30 mins) Can we create and perform an under-the-sea dance?

What you need and preparation

In the classroom, discuss with the children the opening and closing actions of sea anemones.

You will need: a CD or tape player; 'Waltz of the Flowers' from Tchaikovsky's *Nutcracker Suite*; video recording and viewing equipment (optional).

What to do

(5 mins) Warm-up

Remind the children how to play the starfish statues game. Play the game, practising the shapes:

- Crabs – in pairs, back to back, holding each other's hands between legs.
- Octopus – in fours with eight waving limbs.
- Shipwreck – in threes, making a sharp jagged shape.

Ask the children for one or two more ideas to add. (For example, limpets could be a still shape on all fours with bottom in the air.)

(8 mins) Development

Ask the children to stretch and reach with one hand, using all the space around them. Encourage them to keep this smooth and flowing and to use spaces in front of them, to their sides, behind them, high up and low down to the accompaniment ('Waltz of the Flowers'). Ask them to try using the other hand and then to try, from a sitting or lying position, using one leg then the other.

Just using their trunks, ask them to try a similar flowing, bending stretching movement.

Now tell the children to sit in groups of four and to decide between them how they can open and close like an anemone. Listen to an extract from 'Waltz of the Flowers', then practise together opening and closing in time to the music. Encourage the children to listen to the phrases and time their movements accordingly.

(14 mins) Dance

Choose parts of the dances from the last few sessions to put together into a sequence. Provide a clear accompaniment, and you could ask the children to choose which parts they want to do. Let the children practise and refine the sequences.

Video the performances if you have the time and resources.

(3 mins) Cool-down

Ask the children to shake their arms, legs, then the whole body. Tell them to stretch slowly to reach into the air and then curl up small before returning to the classroom.

Classroom review

As a class, discuss what have been the favourite moments over the last few weeks. What did the children think they did best? Where could they have made improvements?

If you made a video of the final performances, watch it together as a class, and use it to provoke a more in-depth analysis of the last few weeks.

Assessing learning outcomes

Can the children remember the actions from the last few weeks? Are they able to demonstrate an awareness of the different qualities? Can they respond to the different forms of accompaniment?

Learning objectives
- Remember, repeat and link actions from the last few weeks.
- Demonstrate awareness of the different qualities of the actions.
- Respond appropriately to different forms of accompaniment and use different pathways.

Lesson organisation
Classroom discussion; individual warm-up; individual and group practice; individual cool-down; teacher-led classroom review.

Gymnastics

In order to help children fully explore the potential of their bodies through gymnastics, it is necessary to suggest some challenges or place some limitations in movement. By providing a clear focus of attention, children can be involved in thinking about, performing and adapting their movements to the different suggestions. It is this response to movement problems which is so important. Children need time to play with ideas, to practise, consolidate and refine their favourite movements as well as to have new ones suggested to them. To explore the potential of different ideas and themes is a highly formative process of exploration and discovery. Children are all individual and will come to each session with very different interests, past experiences, abilities and physiques. Challenge is part of the interest and excitement, and a lot is dependent upon your interest and manner.

Progression, therefore, should be seen in a number of dimensions, not simply in the achievements of set gymnastics skills, but also with increasing awareness of their own body, of others and of safety, developing observational skills and increasing quality.

The following themes have been chosen to help children to focus on different gymnastic actions:

● travelling, with particular emphasis on direction
● balancing, with an emphasis on size and shape
● pushing and pulling, which will emphasise these actions in both travelling and balancing.

Exploration and development of these ideas in each unit of work will help children to increase their movement vocabulary in gymnastics by encouraging and challenging them to think of different ways in which they can answer the task set or trying specific suggested actions.

By developing a theme gradually over a series of lessons, children can be helped to build up both confidence and competence and be encouraged to respond imaginatively to the task. The limited focus will help the children to be clear about what they are trying to do and how they are doing it, as well as giving them scope for individual responses, whatever their ability.

Within each lesson, tasks have been selected for introduction or repetition as necessary, depending upon the children's responses. Attempts have been made to ensure that there is a balance between the introduction of new ideas and the choice and practise of familiar movements, and parts of the body used. Demonstrations can be chosen from the children's responses to illustrate range of ideas (to increase variety), use of space, and quality.

Linking movements

At the end of floor work and/or apparatus parts of the lesson, children can be asked to choose their favourite actions from those which they have been trying out or practising. In the early stages of learning to link actions, this will be an important part of them using their initiative and becoming more independent in their choices. It gives them the opportunity to choose actions with which they are competent and which they enjoy performing. This will build up confidence and help them practise and refine the actions that they have chosen. As they progress, they can then be asked to select actions that answer the task set. For example, one way of travelling sideways on their hands and feet or one way of balancing on a large part of their body. This will begin to encourage them to remember and refine moves which they can later include in a short sequence. For example, one way of balancing on a part of their body, making a large shape and one way of balancing on two hands and two feet making a small shape.

Thus children become involved in the process of choosing, selecting, planning and practising and combining, and can begin to think of and try different ways of linking actions together.

Apparatus

Types of apparatus available

These include: mats; benches – padded, wooden, metal; planks and fixings; A-frames; padded platforms, trestle-tables and box-tops; soft play wedges; fixed climbing apparatus – foldaway, cave Southampton; climbing units – ropes, rope ladders, spider's web.

Organisation of apparatus

Make a plan of the apparatus to be used and make sure that what is available will support the theme.

It is essential that the principle of having resources ready and easily accessible, with clear routines for getting out and putting away (similar to those adopted in the classroom) is used in PE. Divide the class into four or six groups (to ensure all the children have a range of experiences and to help spacing). Each group should be responsible for handling the same apparatus each lesson. (Change over each term or half term.)

Establish a fair and logical pattern of rotation of groups. For example, zigzag or clockwise (or straight swap if there are groups with similar apparatus).

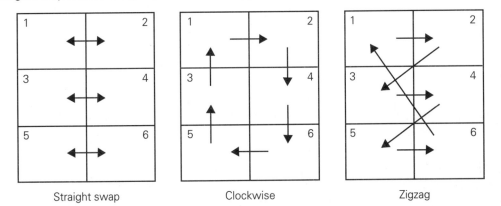

Straight swap   Clockwise   Zigzag

The zigzag is recommended so that groups use different types of apparatus in a lesson (for example part of the climbing apparatus and some portable apparatus). This will ensure that, over several lessons, the children can fully explore each group of apparatus. (NB. There should be a maximum of two apparatus changes in one lesson.) See photocopiable page 160 for further advice.

Teach each group how to get out their apparatus correctly (see the guidelines on the next page), and where to put it. (Use chalk marks initially to indicate the positioning of apparatus.)

Check the fixings and placement of apparatus before it is used.

Using apparatus

There are two main methods for using apparatus:
- Free use. The children get out and put away the same apparatus but move freely around the whole area, working all the time and not standing waiting for turns. This gives young children the choice to go where they feel confident and to use their initiative in moving and looking for spaces. They will need encouragement to use different parts of the apparatus.
- Groups. This is recommended (particularly when there is a favourite piece of apparatus, for example ropes or climbing frame). Group organisation helps to ensure fair turns and will enable each group of children to have a similar amount of time on each arrangement. Each group will get out and put away their own apparatus but rotate to use other parts of the apparatus.

Whichever method you use:
- establish 'ground rules', for example, ensure that the children work quietly and considerately, using all the space, using the floor as well as the apparatus
- insist on a quiet working atmosphere, but discuss why with the children
- encourage and help the children to share space and equipment (using the floor space around the apparatus), particularly when there is limited apparatus
- establish a consistent routine for stopping, coming down and sitting away from the apparatus.

Children at Key Stage 1 will enjoy the responsibility of lifting and carrying the apparatus and co-operating with their group to make sure it is carefully and safely placed and checked by you and them. It will take time, but can be achieved with practise and perseverance.

To encourage maximum activity and independence, avoid queues and encourage children to use their apparatus independently in different ways (for example using different places to get on and off), thoughtfully, carefully, responsibly and imaginatively.

Guidelines for introducing children to handling apparatus

When children begin learning to lift, carry and take responsibility for handling apparatus, you need to give them clear guidance and direction, emphasising the importance of safety. If possible, enable reception children to briefly watch another class. Photocopiable page 160 could be used as a poster, displayed in the classroom and/or the hall, as a reminder to the children.

Group children in twos then fours, and ask each group to sit together in a space. This can be the spot where they are to put the mat or bench, or these places can be marked with chalk. Ask the first group to demonstrate, emphasising bending the knees and not the back, and all moving facing the same direction. Ensure careful placement, and tuck handles in if necessary. Encourage handling mats in fours, two to each side, rather than one at each corner, as some mats tend to sag.

Mats should be considered as pieces of apparatus (to practise balancing, travelling, rolling and so on), and not just a landing area. This is impossible if mats are placed under or too close to other apparatus such as planks and climbing apparatus. If the focus includes jumping and landing, then mats should be placed specifically to enable safe movement off the apparatus.

Setting up the foldaway apparatus

Most children in Years 1 and 2 should be able to assist in getting some of the apparatus out.

Before using the apparatus, check that the bolt holes are clear and that any attachments are accessible and safely placed. Undo the strap around the foldaway.

Safety is essential, and explanations should focus on what should happen and why it is necessary:

- One child lifts the bolt, pulls the foldaway about a metre away from the wall and pauses.
- Another child joins in to push the foldaway out.
- One child lines up the bolt with the hole and bolts the foldaway to the floor.
- Repeat on the other side. Once practised, both bays could come out together.
- Apparatus fixings are then checked by you and the children.
- The teacher lifts ladders off the bay and fixes them to the main frame.

To become more proficient, it is recommended that one group handle this apparatus regularly for half a term (as with other apparatus).

Three groups (of no more than five per group) can use this apparatus (a bay each), provided that other apparatus (for example benches, mats and planks) are added to help spacing.

Travelling in different ways

This theme will build on children's experiences of finding spaces and travelling on different parts of the body, and will explore moving in different directions on the floor and apparatus. Children will practise with increased control and co-ordination, using the space safely.

Balancing and making shapes

The focus for this series of lessons will help children to become more aware of the tension needed to hold still shapes. Emphasising the size of actions will help children to refine them and begin to think about the shapes they are making.

Pushing and pulling – travelling and balancing

This theme will raise children's awareness of pushing and pulling and allow them to demonstrate their understanding. Using their muscles to push to hold shapes and jump and pull to travel or hold on to apparatus will focus attention on travelling and balancing actions with a different emphasis.

Travelling in different ways

The focus for this series of lessons will develop children's experience of travelling on different parts of their body (for example just feet, hands and feet, other parts of body). The particular emphasis on direction will provide an opportunity for children to explore and practise ways in which they can travel in different directions. It will raise their awareness of the different directions they can move in using both the floor and the apparatus and help to increase their movement vocabulary. It will also help them to become more aware of safety issues – looking before they move, moving into spaces, becoming more aware of others as they move, how they use the apparatus and where they can move on the apparatus. (NB. For safety, the children will need to be taught to look before they move.)

The unit is divided into six sessions, allowing at least 30 minutes of activity per session. Each session will involve both floor and apparatus work, but ideas can be modified to suit individual school contexts. The class could be divided into six groups to ensure good spacing and fair turns on each group of apparatus (see the suggested apparatus plan on photocopiable page 153).

Each group should be responsible for the same apparatus each lesson and, after putting it out, will move to the apparatus they are to work on.

The lesson plans presume that children will have had experience of different ways of travelling on different parts of the body and that their landings are becoming more controlled.

UNIT: Travelling in different ways

Enquiry questions	Learning objectives	Teaching activities	Learning outcomes
What directions can we move in?	● Practise ways of travelling around the hall, thinking about different directions. ● Explore ways of moving around, along and over the floor and benches, using different directions. ● Understand travelling on hands and feet.	Warm-up: walking and running on the spot and around the hall; practising stopping and starting; play 'Statue stops'. Floor work: practising different ways of moving on the feet going forwards and other directions, particularly sideways; moving on all fours forwards and sideways in different ways. Apparatus work: travelling on feet forwards and sideways, using all the space around benches and mats; practising favourite travelling actions along, on and off the apparatus, thinking about direction. Cool-down: lying on the floor, tensing and relaxing the body.	Children: ● begin to think about directions, particularly forwards and sideways ● move carefully on all fours with their hands flat ● use the space well on the floor and on the apparatus
How can we travel sideways?	● Practise ways of travelling on different parts of the feet in different ways and in different directions. ● Explore ways of travelling on the body – on the floor and on the apparatus. ● Select and try ways of travelling forwards and sideways on large apparatus. ● Learn to lift and carry apparatus in groups.	Warm-up: tiptoeing on the spot and around the hall; practising 'Stop and go'; playing 'Traffic lights'. Floor work: moving on different parts of the feet, forwards and sideways; practising bouncy jumps sideways; exploring ways of travelling on the body, using different parts and moving in different directions. Apparatus work: travelling actions all around the apparatus; trying sideways movements using feet and other body parts; practising favourite travelling actions using different directions. Cool-down: relaxing (floppy); stretching, relaxing and curling up.	● are mindful of the space and other people ● use different parts of their bodies to move on in different directions ● describe what they have done
What other ways of travelling sideways can we try?	● Practise ways of travelling on feet moving sideways. ● Practise ways of using two hands and two feet to move sideways on the floor and on the apparatus. ● Try rolling sideways. ● Practise lifting, carrying, placing and using apparatus safely. ● Practise moving in different directions on the apparatus.	Warm-up: jogging on the spot and around the space; playing 'Traffic lights'; practising side-stepping. Floor work: choosing ways of travelling sideways; practising side-step; practising moving sideways on all fours and then the body; trying side 'log' roll; in pairs, showing favourite sideways actions. Apparatus work: trying sideways actions using all parts of the apparatus; resting on bodies, moving around the apparatus; trying sideways rolls on floor and mats; rotating to try these on the next apparatus; practising two travelling actions. Cool-down: curling, stretching and relaxing.	● move sideways ● space well on the apparatus ● lift, carry, place and use equipment safely
Can we bunny jump and roll sideways?	● Try bunny jumps, moving forwards and sideways. ● Practise tucked sideways roll. ● Think about ways of getting on and off apparatus. ● Select and try ways of travelling in different directions, particularly sideways, on several parts of the apparatus.	Warm-up: bouncing forwards, backwards, side to side and on the spot; making a pattern of jumps, repeating and practising. Floor work: Jumping and landing on the spot and moving sideways; moving sideways on hands and feet; practising bunny jumps on the spot and travelling forwards and sideways; practising long-side roll then curled side roll; practising linking together favourite travelling actions in different directions. Apparatus work: moving about forwards and sideways using all the apparatus; finding places to bunny jump and side roll; finding different places to get on and off the apparatus, and practising different ways. Cool-down: jumping, getting lower until sitting; stretching out and relax.	● understand and demonstrate travelling in different directionson the floor and apparatus, particularly sideways

Enquiry questions	Learning objectives	Teaching activities	Learning outcomes
How can we refine ways of travelling in different directions?	• Refine bunny-jump actions, moving forwards, sideways and backwards. • Select travelling actions in different directions using different parts of the body and link them into a sequence. • Practise and refine different directions of travel on the apparatus. • Select and try two or three ways of travelling in different directions and link them together.	Warm-up: hopping on the spot then around the hall in different directions; play 'Video'. Floor work: side-stepping; choosing favourite ways of moving sideways then backwards; practising bunny jumps in different directions; trying to link together travelling actions in different directions. Apparatus work: practising ways of travelling from one part of the apparatus to another; practising ways of getting on and off apparatus; using feet, hands and body, starting to link actions together in different directions. Cool-down: tucking up, stretching and relaxing.	• perform a bunny jump safely and carefully • select appropriate actions using different directions for their sequence on the floor and the apparatus
Can we create a sequence for our travelling actions?	• Continue to improve ways of travelling in different directions. • Practise and improve bunny-jump actions in different directions. • Refine and combine ways of travelling in different directions to create a sequence on the floor and on the apparatus.	Warm-up: hopping on the spot and around the hall in different directions; play 'Video'. Floor work: remembering and practising ways of moving in different directions on feet and hands, and feet and body; practising three travelling actions (one in each direction) and linking them into a sequence; thinking about start and finish positions. Apparatus work: refining travelling in different directions and linking them together; performing a sequence to half the class; recognising directions in the actions seen. Cool-down: lying down and relaxing; thinking about how well they performed their sequence.	• demonstrate their knowledge of travelling in different directions by linking their chosen actions into a sequence on the floor and apparatus.

Cross-curricular links
Maths and geography: enhancing children's understanding of directions and spatial awareness.

Resources
Apparatus; photocopiable pages 153 and 160.

Travelling in different
ways

30 **What directions can we move in?**
mins

What you need and preparation

You will need mats and one bench for each of six groups (approximately five children per group).

Discuss with the children in the classroom the special requirements for getting to the hall and doing gymnastics (see Apparatus on page 48 of the introduction to this chapter).

What to do

5 **Warm-up**
mins Ensure the children are well spaced to start the warm-up. Ask them to try little walking and then little running steps on the spot, encouraging light feet with some stretch in the ankle. Start with the toes hardly leaving the floor then gradually encourage the children to lift their feet a little higher off the ground. Ask the children to tiptoe forwards around the hall, in and out of each other, keeping in a big space. Encourage listening by frequently stopping and starting the action.

Play a game of 'Statue stops' to encourage quick responses. Ask the children to travel in and out around the hall but stop still like a statue on your stop signal. (Non-elimination.)

12 **Floor work**
mins Ask the children to choose another way of moving on their feet to practise (for example jumping, hopping), and then another. Practise these ways of travelling on the feet while moving forwards around the hall, encouraging the children to think about spacing and how they could make their action better (for example lighter or slower).

Ask them which other directions they can move in. Encourage them to try the action they just practised in a different direction. Praise travelling actions which move sideways, backwards, diagonally. Choose demonstrations from children's responses to illustrate moving sideways and then ask everyone to try moving sideways.

Ask the class to use their hands and their feet to travel forwards slowly around the hall. Emphasise that they should make sure their hands are flat on the floor and they are looking where they are going. Try different ways – for example, with tummy uppermost or back uppermost. Encourage the children to try the same action in a different direction. Can they go sideways?

Choose two or three children with different ideas to demonstrate travelling sideways on hands and feet (see Diagram 1). Ask everyone to try again. Are they all keeping their hands flat? Are they looking where they are going?

Learning objectives
● Practise ways of travelling around the hall, thinking about different directions.
● Explore ways of moving around, along and over the floor and benches, using different directions.
● Understand travelling on hands and feet.

Lesson organisation
Brief classroom discussion; individual warm-up and floor work; group apparatus practice; individual cool-down; teacher-led classroom review.

Vocabulary
sideways
forwards
backwards
statues
weaving in and out
walking
running
jogging
jumping

Diagram 1

Travelling in different ways

Apparatus work

10 mins Ask each group to put out one mat and one bench in a space (see Apparatus beginning on page 48).

Tell the children to move forwards on their feet around their bench or mat and to practise some of the ways of travelling they tried earlier in the lesson (such as walking, jogging and hopping). Emphasise towards, away from, along, over or around the bench. Encourage them to move sideways as well as forwards. Insist that they look for spaces and keep moving.

Suggest to the children that they travel on all fours (hands and feet), and encourage varied use of the bench and the space around it (for example along the bench, across the floor or mat, under the bench, around or away from the bench). Look for good examples of the different possibilities to use as demonstrations to suggest ideas to other children. Use demonstrations to illustrate two or three ways. Then encourage the rest of the children all to try the same action travelling sideways, then to try a different way (see Diagram 2).

For the last few minutes, ask the children to choose and practise their favourite travelling actions and to think about which direction they are moving in. Encourage them to choose two actions in two different directions (forwards and sideways).

Diagram 2

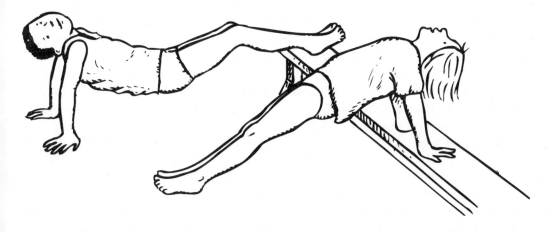

Cool-down

3 mins Ask the children to lie down in a space and to make a still shape. Tell them to hold their body tense and tight like a statue and then relax and make their body go all floppy. Ask them to try another shape and repeat.

Classroom review
Encourage the children to talk about and describe some of the travelling actions they tried. Ask:
● Which travelling actions did you choose?
● Which directions did you travel in?
● What did you have to remember?

Assessing learning outcomes
Are the children beginning to think about directions, particularly forwards and sideways? Are they moving carefully on all fours with their hands flat? Are they using the space well on the floor and on the apparatus?

Travelling in different
ways

30 mins How can we travel sideways?

Learning objectives
● Practise ways of travelling on different parts of the feet in different ways and in different directions, particularly sideways.
● Explore ways of travelling on the body – on the floor and on the apparatus.
● Select and try ways of travelling forwards and sideways on large apparatus.
● Learn to lift and carry apparatus in groups.

Lesson organisation
Classroom discussion; individual warm-up; floor work and apparatus work in six groups; individual cool-down; teacher-led classroom review in pairs.

What you need and preparation

You will need apparatus accessible for each of six groups (approximately five children per group); the apparatus plan on photocopiable page 153.

Discuss with children in the classroom the special requirements for getting out the apparatus (see page 48 and photocopiable page 160).

What to do

4 mins **Warm-up**

Ask children to tiptoe on the spot, lightly lifting the feet and pointing the toes, and then to move forwards around the hall. Check their spacing and encourage them to use small steps, moving forwards and then sideways, always into spaces. Practise stop and go by playing 'Statues'. Develop this into a traffic lights game with:

● Red – still.
● Green – tiptoe around.
● Amber – tiptoe on the spot.

If the children are responding well, add the following: on the signal *Change*, ask them to change from forwards to sideways or vice versa.

8 mins **Floor work**

Ask the class to try moving forwards on another part of their feet (heels or sides), then to try the same way moving sideways.

On the spot, ask them to try little bounces on the balls of their feet, lightly bending the hips, knees and ankles to practise safe landings. Ask a few children for demonstrations.

Ask everyone to bounce sideways around the hall. Try to the left and to the right. (This could be done with everyone facing you to begin with.)

Now tell the children to lie down. This could be on their backs, sides or fronts. Ask them what they must remember to do before they move. (Look for spaces.) Encourage them to move into another space on the part of their body on which they are lying by sliding or pushing. Help them to become aware of which part of the body is touching the floor and then to try to move on that same part in another direction. (See Diagram 3.)

Use a few examples for demonstration and then encourage everyone to try out and practise one of those ideas or a new way of their own.

Vocabulary
forwards
sideways
backwards
statues
tiptoes
bounces
lifting
carrying
freeze

Diagram 3

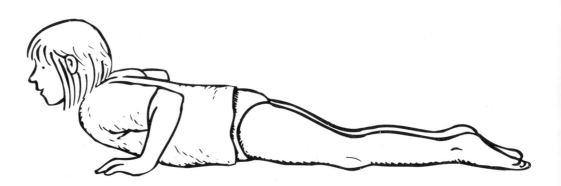

Travelling in different ways

(15 mins) Apparatus work

Using the apparatus notes and plan, organise the children into six groups and allocate apparatus to each group. Explain to each group how to get out their particular apparatus.

Ask the children to try out some of the travelling actions on their feet they have tried in these two lessons: towards, away from, along, over or around their group's apparatus (for example on tiptoes, walking, bouncing). Insist on always looking for spaces and keeping moving. Encourage the use of sideways as well as forwards movement.

Ask the class to use their bodies (backs, sides, fronts, bottoms) to travel along, under or around parts of the apparatus and then to do that moving in different directions. Reinforce a thoughtful use of space.

Look for different possibilities to use as demonstrations to suggest ideas or to challenge other children. Encourage everyone to try moving sideways and to think about the different ways they can do this.

Choose and practise two favourite travelling actions (different directions) and try them one after the other. Check that they are using two different directions.

(3 mins) Cool-down

To finish, ask the children to lie down and relax and make their bodies go all floppy. Then tell them to stretch their arms and legs as wide as possible and relax again. Tell them to curl up the body as small as possible. Stess that you want them to do this slowly. Repeat the whole process several times.

Classroom review

Encourage the children to describe some of the actions they tried to a partner. Prompt them to think about any new action they tried or what they liked doing best.

- What did you like doing best?
- How do you think you improved that travelling action?
- Did you try anything new?
- Was it easier to move sideways in some positions than others?

Differentiation

Some children will need extra help in sharing the space and the apparatus, and suggestions like getting down and getting back on again or moving to another part of their apparatus which is free will support them.

More able children can be encouraged to think about and refine the shapes of their actions.

Assessing learning outcomes

Are the children mindful of the space and other people? Have they used different parts of their bodies to move on in different directions? Can they describe what they have done?

30 mins What other ways of travelling sideways can we try?

Learning objectives
● Practise ways of travelling on the feet moving sideways.
● Practise ways of using two hands and two feet to move sideways on the floor and on the apparatus.
● Try rolling sideways on the body.
● Practise lifting, carrying, placing and using apparatus safely.
● Practise moving in different directions on the apparatus.

Lesson organisation
Brief teacher-led classroom discussion; individual warm-up; individual and paired floor work; apparatus practice in six groups; teacher-led classroom review.

Vocabulary
jogging
faster
slower
side-step

What you need and preparation

You will need apparatus ready at the sides for each of six groups (approximately five children per group). See the apparatus plan on photocopiable page 153.

Discuss in the classroom the special requirements for getting out apparatus (see Apparatus in the chapter introduction and photocopiable page 160) and moving on to the next apparatus.

What to do

3 mins Warm-up

Ask the children to try jogging on the spot, encouraging faster and slower actions. Encourage gradually lifting the knees and then moving carefully around the hall. Encourage moving in different directions, sideways then backwards (looking where they are going).

Play 'Traffic lights' using jogging:
● Green – jog.
● Red – stop.
● Amber – jog on the spot.
● Change – change direction.

10 mins Floor work

Ask the children to choose a way of travelling on their feet, moving sideways, and refine this. Ask everyone to try one or two of the children's ideas, then teach the side-step. (Explain that the body stays facing one direction; starting to the left, left foot reaches out to the left and then right foot closes up; left foot reaches out to the left and right foot closes up again – no crossing of feet.)

Ask one or two of the children to demonstrate this movement or show it to the class yourself. Then encourage everyone to try side-stepping into spaces, changing direction every few steps. Check on the children's use of space.

Let everyone practise this, sometimes moving sideways one way and sometimes the other way. Ask the children to try another way of travelling sideways on their feet (such as jogging, jumping or hopping).

Then ask them to practise moving sideways on two hands and two feet. Advise them to try one way in one direction, then one way in another direction (walking, side-stepping; tummy upwards , back upwards and so on).

Now tell them to try moving sideways on large parts of their bodies (for example sides, bottoms, backs). Use a few good examples for demonstration and then encourage all the children to try a new way of their own.

Finally, ask all the children to lie down on their backs in a space in a long thin shape with their arms stretched above their heads. Ask them to roll over onto their fronts smoothly and gently, keeping well stretched, and then to roll from their fronts onto their backs (log roll). Encourage them to practise this roll smoothly and carefully.

In pairs, children could show each other one of their sideways actions (using feet, hands and feet or other areas of the body) and suggest how they could be improved (for example using greater control or making a clearer shape).

14 mins Apparatus work

Using the apparatus notes and the plan on photocopiable page 153, put the children into their six groups. Ask them to set up their allocated apparatus, then to point and then move to their next apparatus and space out.

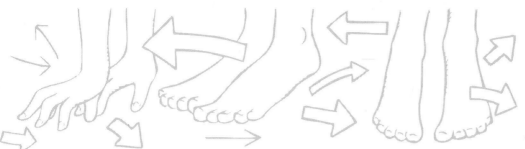

Ask the children to try out some of the sideways travelling actions they have tried so far: towards, away from, along, over or around their group's apparatus. Insist that they look for spaces and keep moving.

Ask the class to rest on their bodies to move themselves along, under or around parts of the apparatus, for example rolling, sliding, pushing, pulling or wriggling (see Diagram 4).

Diagram 4

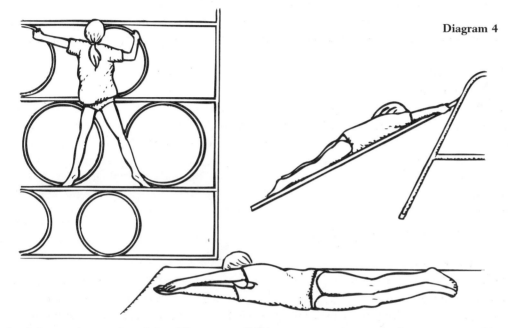

Look for good examples of the different possibilities to use as demonstrations to suggest ideas or to challenge other children. Encourage good control of actions.

Can the children try a sideways roll on the mat or anywhere else? Finish off by asking the children to select and practise two travelling actions moving in different directions (preferably using different parts of the body).

Rotate to new apparatus and try out the above tasks on this apparatus.

3 mins **Cool-down**
Ask the children to curl up small on any part of their bodies and hold the shape still for a few seconds, then stretch out slowly and move onto another part to make another curled shape. Tell them to stretch out, relax and let their bodies go floppy.

Differentiation

Encourage more able children to refine and clarify their actions and to try new ways to respond to the tasks.

Encourage less able children to have a go at the actions, giving them practical teaching points and suggestions.

Classroom review

Ask the children: *What actions did you learn to do sideways today? What did you enjoy most?*

Assessing learning outcomes

Are the children understanding and moving sideways? Which are the easiest movements to do sideways? Are they spacing well on the apparatus? Do they know how to lift, carry, place and use equipment safely?

(30 mins) Can we bunny jump and roll sideways?

Learning objectives
● Try bunny jumps, moving forwards and sideways.
● Practise the tucked sideways roll.
● Think about ways of getting on and off apparatus.
● Select and try ways of travelling in different directions, particularly sideways, on several parts of the apparatus.

Lesson organisation
Teacher-led classroom discussion; individual warm-up and floor work; apparatus work in six groups; teacher-led classroom review.

Vocabulary
bunny jump
tucked
stretched
linking

What you need and preparation
Arrange apparatus to be ready for six groups (approximately five children per group). Have a copy of the apparatus plan on photocopiable page 153 to hand.

Discuss beforehand the particular requirements for getting out the apparatus (see page 48 and photocopiable page 160) and for moving on to use the next apparatus.

What to do

(3 mins) Warm-up
Ask the children to try little bounces and jumps forwards and backwards and then from side to side on the spot. Emphasise light, squashy landings.

Encourage them to make a pattern of jumps and to practise and repeat the pattern. This will raise the pulse and help them to use different directions. See if they can remember a simple pattern of jumps.

Diagram 5

(10 mins) Floor work
Ask the children to practise jumping and landing on the spot and then to practise jumping sideways into a big space.

Now ask them to recall and practise some ways of moving on their hands and feet using different directions, including sideways.

Select a child trying a bunny-jump idea. Ask them to demonstrate, then encourage all the children to practise a bunny jump on the spot, checking that their hands are flat and their arms straight.

Let the children practise bunny jumps, moving forwards and then encourage them to try sideways and backwards.

Remind them of the stretched sideways roll they tried last session and ask them to practise this smoothly.

Then encourage them to curl up small and to try rolling sideways in a tucked shape (hands tucked into the sides – see Diagram 5).

Now ask the children to choose some of their favourite travelling actions showing different directions. For example, one forwards, one sideways and one backwards.

Finally, before they move on to the apparatus, ask the children to decide which action they want to start with and which one to finish with and then to link them all together smoothly one after the other.

(15 mins) Apparatus work
In their six groups, ask the children to get out their allocated apparatus. (This may be done group by group or a few groups at a time.) Ask them to point and then move to their next apparatus and space out ready to begin.

Travelling in different
ways

Ask the children to move about and use all of their apparatus, using forwards and sideways directions. Encourage good spacing and use of all parts of the apparatus including the mats and the floor. Can they find places where they can bunny jump or roll sideways?

Tell the children to find different places to get on and off their apparatus. Encourage them to think about ways they can try to get on forwards, sideways or even backwards.

Encourage them to explore ways of climbing down, getting off the apparatus with a little jump or bunny jump action, thinking about the direction in which they are moving. Ask:
● Which direction are you moving in?
● Can you think of another way of doing that?
● Can you still do that moving in another direction?

Encourage the children to select and practise different ways of getting on and off and travelling on parts of the apparatus, thinking about different directions.

Rotate to the next apparatus and try out the above tasks on that apparatus.

2 mins Cool-down
Ask the children to jump on the spot, slowly getting lower and lower and then to rise up slowly. Repeat this jumping, getting lower until they can sit down in a curled shape. Check that they are doing this slowly and carefully and then ask them to stretch out along the floor in a long thin shape and relax. Let them repeat this once more.

Classroom review
Ask the children to think about the different directions and ways they got on and off the apparatus. Ask them to describe these to a partner.

Assessing learning outcomes
Can the children understand and demonstrate travel in various directions on the floor and apparatus, particularly sideways?

30 mins Can we refine ways of travelling in different directions?

What you need and preparation
Organise apparatus for each of six groups (approximately five children per group) – see the apparatus plan on photocopiable page 153.

Remind the children in the classroom of the requirements for getting out the apparatus (see page 48 and photocopiable page 160) and ask them to remember some of the travelling actions in different directions that they have tried in previous sessions.

What to do
4 mins Warm-up
Ask the children to hop on the spot (changing legs after a while) and then to hop around the hall. Encourage a stronger hop and use of the arms to hop higher and then to hop a greater distance. Advise them to use different directions.

Introduce and play the video game:
● Stop – stay still.
● Pause – jog on the spot.
● Play – jog steadily.
● Fast forward – faster jog
● Rewind – jog slowly backwards.

Learning objectives
● Refine bunny-jump actions, moving forwards, sideways and backwards.
● Select travelling actions in different directions using different parts of the body and link them into a sequence.
● Practise and refine different directions of travel on the apparatus.
● Select and try two or three ways of travelling in different directions and link them together.

CHAPTER 2 GYMNASTICS

Travelling in different ways

(10 mins) Floor work

Ask the children to practise side-stepping, moving first to one side, then the other. Give frequent instructions to change direction. Then ask them to choose their favourite way(s) of travelling sideways and to clarify the action. Then ask them to choose and practise their favourite way of travelling backwards. Watch for carefully controlled actions.

Remind the children of the bunny jump action and allow them a few minutes to practise them moving forwards, sideways and backwards.

Ask the children to select two or three ways of travelling in different directions and to practise linking them together.

Encourage them with prompts about using different parts of their bodies and including at least two different directions.

(15 mins) Apparatus work

In groups, ask the children to get out their allocated apparatus. Ask them to point to and then move to their next apparatus and space out ready to begin.

In their groups, ask the children to find different ways of travelling in different directions, moving from one part of the apparatus to another (across the mat, over or along the bench, onto and across the climbing apparatus).

Ask the children to find places where they can jump to get on or off the apparatus – using hands or feet (forwards, backwards and sideways).

Encourage them to choose and practise travelling actions in different directions and to try ways of linking them together.

Ask them which other parts of the apparatus they could use in their sequences. Ask everyone: *Have you used all parts of your apparatus?*

Then tell all the groups to rotate to the next apparatus and space out. Try out the above tasks on that apparatus.

(1 min) Cool-down

Ask the children to tuck up small and then to stretch out and relax. Repeat the sequence.

Classroom review

Ask the children to think about the directions that they chose or could choose to link together to make a sequence and to remember them for the next lesson.

Assessing learning outcomes

Can the children perform a bunny jump? Can they do it safely and carefully? Are they selecting appropriate actions and using different directions for their sequence on the floor and the apparatus?

Can we create a sequence for our travelling directions?

(30 mins)

What you need and preparation

You will need apparatus for each of six groups (approximately five children per group) – see the apparatus plan on photocopiable page 153.

Remind the children of the requirements for getting out apparatus (see pages 48 and 160).

What to do

(5 mins) Warm-up

Ask the children to hop on the spot and then around the hall, sometimes forwards, sometimes sideways and sometimes backwards.

Play 'Video' from the previous lesson (see page 61).

(8 mins) Floor work

Ask the children to choose one way of moving around the hall on their feet (hop, jump, jog, skip and so on) and to practise travelling in different directions. Encourage them to keep moving and to keep changing direction, always looking for spaces.

See if they can remember some of the ways they moved on their hands and feet or on their bodies in the previous lessons and let them practise these, going in different directions.

Ask everyone to select and practise their three favourite travelling actions, one in each direction, and link them together smoothly to make a sequence on the floor. Encourage them to think what direction and action they want to start with and to show you their starting position. Ask them to stand up or keep still when they have finished their sequence to show you their finishing position.

Allow them a few minutes to practise and refine their sequences.

(15 mins) Apparatus work

In groups, ask the children to get out their allocated apparatus. Ask them to point to and then move to their next apparatus and space out ready to begin.

Ask them to select and practise travelling actions (one for each direction) and to link them together in a sequence using different parts of the apparatus and different parts of their bodies. Where could they start on their apparatus?

Watch half the class perform their sequences first. Help the viewers to recognise and identify the directions they can see in the sequences. Swap over and watch the other half of the class.

(2 mins) Cool-down

Ask the children to lie down in a space and let their whole body relax. Encourage them to think about how well they performed their sequences.

Classroom review

What did the class like about the sequences they observed? Ask them to focus on direction, good use of space, controlled actions, smoothly linked actions or good starting and finishing positions.

Differentiation

Some children will need help and prompts to clearly remember and refine their actions.

Assessing learning outcomes

Can the children demonstrate their knowledge of travelling in different directions by linking their chosen actions into a sequence on the floor and apparatus?

Learning objectives
● Continue to improve ways of travelling in different directions.
● Practise and improve bunny-jump actions in different directions.
● Refine and combine ways of travelling in different directions to create a sequence on the floor and on the apparatus.

Lesson organisation
Teacher-led classroom discussion; individual warm-up and floor work; apparatus work in six groups; teacher-led classroom review.

Vocabulary
combine
link
sequence

Follow-up activity
Display photographs of the children's gymnastic actions under 'Travelling in different directions'.

Balancing and making shapes

This unit will help children to develop the body awareness and tension which is required to hold the body in stillness over an increasingly smaller base on the floor and on apparatus. The particular focus for this series of lessons is static balance on large patches and smaller parts of the body. At this early stage in the development of their balancing skills, the emphasis will be on stillness and size of shape.

Children will be encouraged to balance using different parts of their body, their feet or their hands and feet. It is helpful to start with large patches (sides, backs, fronts, bottoms) or all fours so that they can be successful in feeling stability and in controlling their bodies. The size or the number of parts used can gradually be reduced, encouraging children to balance on smaller bases. There will be wide variations in the ways in which they can be challenged to do this.

An added dimension to this unit will emphasise large and small shapes. This will help children to become aware of size and shape as they balance, and assist them in refining their actions.

An emphasis on balance can result in a rather static lesson, therefore, children should be encouraged to travel between balances, particularly when they start to link balancing actions together.

The unit is divided into six sessions, allowing 30–40 minutes of activity in each session. All sessions involve both floor and apparatus work, but ideas can be modified to suit individual contexts. The class could be divided into six groups to ensure good spacing and fair turns on each group of apparatus. Each group will be responsible for handling the same apparatus each lesson – see the Apparatus section in the chapter introduction. A suggested apparatus plan is provided on photocopiable page 154.

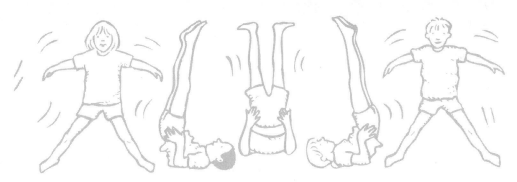

UNIT: Balancing and making shapes

Enquiry questions	Learning objectives	Teaching activities	Learning outcomes
Can we balance and make large shapes?	● Practise ways of travelling on feet with emphasis on large and small steps, using two feet or one foot. ● Explore and practise using large parts of the body to rest on to hold large shapes on the floor, benches and mats. ● Explore still shapes on all fours on the floor, benches and mats. ● Try out and practise large, still shapes on two feet. ● Co-operate with a group to lift, carry, place and use one bench and one mat safely.	Warm-up: walking then jogging in different directions using large and small steps; choosing other ways of moving on feet; playing 'Large and small'; practising holding the body tight to keep still. Floor work: lying down on different large parts of the body, making shapes then emphasising wide shapes; practising stretching and combining two large shapes on large parts of the body; lifting part of the body off the ground; trying a bottom balance; practising different shapes with the legs; practising favourite balances. Apparatus work: walking in and out of the bench and mat using small and large steps; making large shapes on the mat, floor or bench; demonstrating good spacing; practising favourite still shapes on different parts of the apparatus. Cool-down: making little jumps on the spot; tiptoeing around the hall and then on the spot.	Children: ● understand the idea of stillness ● use the space well ● handle benches and mats sensibly
Can we make large shapes on all fours?	● Practise ways of travelling on feet with emphasis on large and small actions. ● Explore and practise using large patches of the body to rest on, to hold large and small still shapes. ● Develop and practise a variety of large, still shapes on all fours and on two feet. ● Co-operate within a group to lift, carry, place and use apparatus safely.	Warm-up: walking then jogging on the spot and around the hall; practising stopping and starting; hopping large and small hops; choosing other travelling actions; practising still, large shapes on feet; playing 'Large and small'. Floor work: practising different still shapes on all fours, high and low; practising different still shapes on two feet in different ways; stretching towards splits. Apparatus work: making still shapes on different parts of the apparatus, using travelling actions to move from one part to another; balancing on large and small parts of the body on the apparatus; making large and small shapes. Cool-down practising little jumps with soft landings; tiptoeing slowly to a stop.	● imaginatively try different still shapes ● keep still for the count of three ● begin to clarify their shapes ● listen to instructions for handling apparatus ● co-operate to get out the apparatus
Can we make still shapes on two hands and one foot?	● Practise making still shapes on two hands and one foot. ● Practise tensing to keep the body very still. ● Explore and practise using large patches of the body to rest on to hold small, still shapes on apparatus. ● Explore and practise making large and small still shapes on apparatus. ● Practise and develop shapes on all fours.	Warm-up: jogging then striding around the hall using large strides; practising pigeon steps and giant strides; playing 'Large and small'. Floor work: practising still shapes on all fours, then on two hands and one foot, one hand and two feet; practising keeping still; refining favourite balances with travelling in between. Apparatus work: making a variety of still shapes on different parts of the apparatus; balancing on large parts of the body on apparatus, then smaller parts; trying large shapes; practising favourite balances. Cool-down: making little hops on the spot; tiptoeing around the space; stretching and curling to relax.	● take their weight on two hands and one foot ● begin to clarify the shapes of their balances ● are aware of others ● space well on the apparatus

UNIT: Balancing and making shapes

Enquiry questions	Learning objectives	Teaching activities	Learning outcomes
Can we make shapes using smaller parts of the body?	● Explore and practise using smaller parts of the body to balance on the floor and apparatus. ● Explore and practise shapes on bottom and shoulders and other small parts of the body. ● Explore and practise still shapes on two hands and one foot, and on one foot.	Warm-up: jogging, then striding around the space using big steps or jumps; practising pigeon steps and giant strides; playing 'Large or small'. Floor work: practising favourite still shapes, emphasising large parts and large shapes, large parts and small shapes to focus on size; trying out still shapes on different small parts of the body and on one foot. Apparatus work: practising making large and small still shapes on large parts of the body, using apparatus imaginatively. Cool-down: skipping on the spot then around the space; skipping in slow motion; stretching and curling to relax.	● use smaller parts of their bodies ● distinguish between small and large parts ● distinguish between small and large shapes
Can we link our balances?	● Practise balancing on one foot, clarifying the shape of the non-weight-bearing leg. ● Explore a combination of small parts to balance on. ● Select, practise and refine several balances to incorporate into a sequence. ● Start to link balances together to form a sequence on the floor and apparatus. ● Comment constructively on a partner's linked balances.	Warm-up: walking, skipping, and galloping around the space in different directions, lifting knees high; playing 'Simon says'. Floor work: practising favourite still shapes; practising balancing on one foot; using a combination of small parts to balance on; linking together two or three shapes with a travelling action in between; observing partners and criticising constructively. Apparatus work: consolidating balances with travelling actions in between on different parts of the apparatus; developing a sequence linking balances with a travelling action in between; practising, showing partner, then practising again. Cool-down: skipping on the spot and around the space; slow-motion stretching and curling to relax.	● comment constructively on their partners' balances ● suggest ideas for improvement ● use a combination of small parts of the body to balance on
Can we improve our sequence of balances?	● Practise and refine a sequence on the floor and apparatus.	Warm-up: walking then striding around the space using large and small steps; playing 'Simon says'. Floor work: practising favourite still shapes using large and small parts of the body and linking them together. Apparatus work: practising different-sized balances on different parts of the apparatus; practising joining them together smoothly. Cool-down: moving around on all fours; shaking the body; relaxing and reflecting on the sequences.	● perform a variety of balances using both the floor and the apparatus ● repeat and refine a sequence of linked actions ● share the space with others safely and fairly.

Cross-curricular links
Science: using and tensing muscles to hold still shapes; looking at stability and size.

Resources
Apparatus; photocopiable pages 154 and 160.

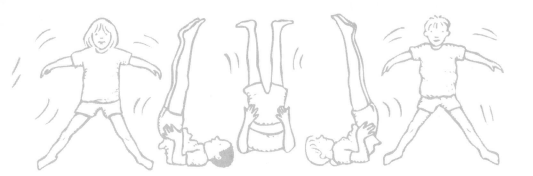

**Balancing and
making shapes**

(40 mins) Can we balance and make large shapes?

What you need and preparation

You will need one bench and one mat for each of six groups.

Discuss with the children in the classroom the requirements for getting to the hall and doing gymnastics (see page 48 and the diagrams on photocopiable page 160).

What to do

(5 mins) Warm-up

Ask the children to walk on the spot and then briskly around the hall, using all the space. Encourage good use of arms and movement in different directions. Introduce using small steps and then large steps. Alternate large and small steps, checking that the children are responding with the appropriate size of actions. Repeat this together, jogging.

Ask the children to choose, then practise, another way of travelling on their feet (for example jumping or hopping) as they move about. Encourage them to look where they are going and to move into spaces.

Ask them to try this action by making large then small steps or jumps. Make a game of this with these instructions:

- Large – large steps or jumps.
- Small – small steps or jumps.
- Stop – stop still like a statue.

Encourage good spacing. Draw attention to gripping and holding the body tight to stay still.

When they are warm, ask the children to think about the different shapes they could make on two feet and then to try one of those still shapes (see Diagram 6, for example). Help them to clarify the shape they are making (such as by stretching a bit more, fingers pointed) and then to try other shapes they can make on two feet (long and thin, wide, curled, and so on).

Repeat the game 'Large and small'. This time on *Stop*, the children should make one of these still shapes on two feet.

Diagram 6

(12 mins) Floor work

Ask the children to lie down (on their backs, sides or tummies) and to think what large parts of the body they are resting on. Encourage them to make a clear shape on that part (tucked or wide) and to hold the shape still for a count of three. Still on that part, ask them to make a wider shape. Let them try out and practise several ways of using large parts and making large shapes.

Tell the children to turn over or rest on another large part of the body and to make another large, still shape (see Diagram 7 on page 68). Move around, looking at the shapes of arms and legs and encourage a good stretch. Use demonstrations to illustrate a variety of the children's ideas. Encourage tension in the body – holding that shape very still for the count of three, before relaxing and trying again. Encourage them to choose and practise two different large shapes on large parts of their body one after the other.

Encourage the children to try lifting part of their bodies off the ground to make a still shape on a smaller base (backs, bottoms, shoulders and so on – see Diagram 8).

Teach a bottom balance (using hands) by asking the children to sit down and place their hands by their hips, just behind their bottom, with fingers facing forwards. Ask them to lift one leg to hold a still shape and then the other leg to hold another still shape. Tell them to lift and stretch both their legs while resting on their hands and their bottom and to think about the shape of their legs in the air. Encourage them to hold the shape still, feeling the tightness in their tummies and then to lower their feet down slowly (see Diagram 9). Try this several times together, making different shapes with the legs.

Diagram 7

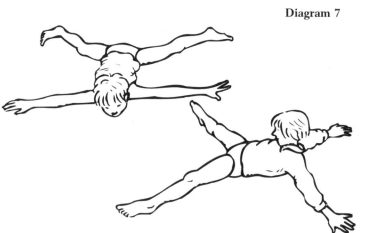

Ask the children to make a still shape on hands and feet (four small parts; tummy or back upwards). Emphasise stillness and check that only hands and feet are touching the floor (see Diagrams 10 and 11). Ask everyone to practise their favourite balances.

18 mins **Apparatus work**
With the children in six groups, ask each group to get out one bench and one mat and to place them separately with a space in between. (See the guidelines for introducing children to handling apparatus on page 50.)

Ask the children to walk, using small steps, in and out of their bench and mat without touching them, always looking for spaces. Then try in and out of all the benches and mats and then return to going in and out of their own bench and mat.

Ask them to try walking using larger strides, this time going across their mat or across or along their bench. Help them to do this making good use of the space.

Ask the children to space out and to find different places on their bench and/or mat or floor space where they can make a large, still shape without being near anyone else. Encourage them to hold the

Diagram 8

Diagram 9

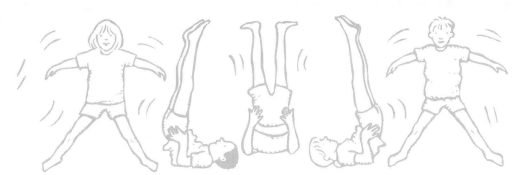

shape still for the count of three and then to travel to a new space (using small strides or choosing a particular travelling action) to make another still shape. Some children will need help looking for spaces. Encourage them to use the floor, the mat and the bench in turn (in any order) to make a still shape. This will help them to spread out. Select and use a demonstration by one group to show good spacing.

Diagram 10

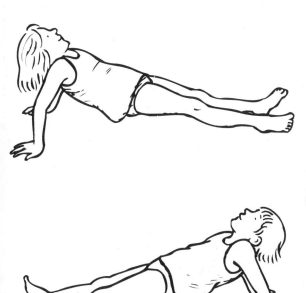

Encourage everyone to use their backs, sides, tummies or bottoms as the base for their shape, and then to use just their hands and feet (on all fours). Part of them could be on the floor and part of them on the mat or bench.

Ask them to choose and practise some of their favourite still shapes on different parts of their apparatus.

To finish, ask the groups to put their apparatus away carefully, one piece at a time.

Cool-down

5 mins When the apparatus is away, ask the children to spread out into the space and to practise lots of little jumps on the spot. Keep an eye out for good squashy landings.

Then instruct the children to slowly tiptoe around the hall in all directions, gradually changing to doing this on the spot and then slowing to a stop.

Classroom review

Ask the children if they have tried to balance on their bottoms before. Could they do this with both feet off the ground? Could they do this without using both hands? What other balances did they try? Could they hold the shapes still?

Differentiation

During the floor work, more able children could be encouraged to try to hold the bottom balance shape without using their hands for support.

Less able children should be encouraged to perform all the activities to the best of their ability. Prompt and encourage their ideas as necessary.

Assessing learning outcomes

Do the children understand the idea of stillness? Are they using the space well? Do they handle the benches and mats sensibly?

Diagram 11

(30 mins) Can we make large shapes on all fours?

What you need and preparation

You will need apparatus accessible at the sides of the hall; an apparatus plan for six groups (see photocopiable page 154).

Discuss with the children the special arrangements for getting out their apparatus (see Apparatus on page 48 and the illustrations on photocopiable page 160).

What to do

(4 mins) Warm-up

Ask the children to walk, then jog on the spot and then around the hall, using all the spaces and stopping still when you say *Stop*.

Ask the children to hop on the spot, first on one foot, then on the other. Then encourage them to do this moving around the hall, keeping their heads up, using their arms to help them hop. Encourage those who can to try large and small hops.

Tell everyone to choose another travelling action on their feet and to try that action again.

When they are warm, ask the children to think about the different large shapes they could make on both feet. Help them to clarify and improve the shape they are making (by stretching a little more, fingers pointed, for example) and then ask them to try small shapes they can make on two feet.

Play the game 'Large and small'. Ask the children to listen and respond to your instructions:
● Large – large steps or jumps.
● Small – small steps or jumps.

Now, instead of jumps, give these instructions for large or small still *shapes* on two feet.

(6 mins) Floor work

Encourage the children to practise several still shapes on all fours (tummy upwards or back upwards). Check that their hands are flat and encourage them to try several different possibilities, selecting some good examples for demonstration. Encourage stillness and check that only their hands and feet are touching the floor.

Ask the children to choose and make a very large, wide shape on all fours. Select a few of the children doing this well to give demonstrations to illustrate varied interpretations of this. Challenge some of the more able children to try their shape with their feet and hands wide and low, or wide and high.

Let everyone practise some of the still shapes on two feet that they made in the warm-up. Emphasise keeping very still and encourage the children to think of different shapes they can make with their feet together (tall or crouched) and then with their feet apart (feet forwards and backwards or feet out to the sides). Encourage stretching out a bit more (towards splits) and then to stretch their arms out as well.

(18 mins) Apparatus work

Organise the children into their six groups, and make sure they know how to get out their apparatus correctly and where to put it. (See the chapter introduction and photocopiable pages 154 and 160.)

Encourage the children to find different places on their apparatus where they can make a still shape. Remind them to use different parts of their apparatus, for example holding on to or resting on parts of the apparatus; tucked around poles or bars; resting on planks, benches or mats or resting on the floor.

Suggest to the children that they choose a space to start and use each part of their apparatus in turn (this will help spacing). For example, one balance on a mat, one balance on a bench, one on a trestle, in any order, always looking for spaces. Encourage small steps, hops or small bunny-jump actions to travel between and around different parts of the apparatus.

Tell the children to balance on a large part of their body, then to move to another part of their apparatus and balance again. Repeat, seeing if they can balance on a smaller part or parts.

Ask them to think about and make large, still shapes on different parts of their apparatus. For example, *holding* on to the apparatus, *hanging* on the apparatus or *resting* on it.

Ask the groups to put away their apparatus one piece at a time.

2
mins **Cool-down**
When the apparatus is away, ask the children to find a space and practise lots of little jumps on the spot. Encourage them to make squashy landings.

Ask them to slowly tiptoe around the hall in all directions, gradually changing to doing this on the spot and slowing to a stop.

Classroom review
Encourage reflection and discussion by asking the children the following questions:
● Which parts of the body did you use to balance on?
● How many parts of your apparatus did you find to balance on?
● You managed to keep really still… What helped you to do this?

Assessing learning outcomes
Are the children imaginatively trying different still shapes? Can they keep still for the count of three? Are they beginning to clarify their shapes? Did they listen to your instructions for lifting and carrying the apparatus? How well did they co-operate to get out the apparatus?

35
mins ## Can we make still shapes on two hands and one foot?

What you need and preparation
You will need apparatus accessible at the sides of the hall; an apparatus plan for six groups (see photocopiable page 154).

Remind the children in the classroom about procedures for handling and using apparatus.

What to do
4
mins **Warm-up**
Ask the children to jog, then stride around the hall, always looking for spaces. Then ask them to try another way of moving on their feet with big steps or jumps.

Ask them to practise pigeon steps and then giant strides, and to alternate the two.

Play 'Large and small' (see pages 67 and 70), asking the children to choose their large or small steps or jumps and make large or small still shapes as you dictate.

Then ask them to choose another way of moving around the hall using other parts of their body.

8
mins **Floor work**
Encourage the children to practise making several different still shapes on all fours. Look for any small shapes to show to the class and then ask them all to try to make some different small shapes (with feet and hands close together; tummy upwards or back upwards and so on). Encourage a variety of responses and select some for demonstration.

Learning objectives
● Practise making still shapes on two hands and one foot.
● Practise tensing to keep the body very still.
● Explore and practise using large patches of the body to rest on to hold small, still shapes on apparatus.
● Explore and practise making large and small still shapes on apparatus.
● Practise and develop shapes on all fours.

Balancing and making shapes

Lesson organisation
Brief classroom discussion; individual warm-up and floor work; six groups to handle and use apparatus; individual cool down; teacher-led classroom review.

Vocabulary
pigeon steps
giant strides

Tell the children to lift one foot off the ground and to make a still shape on two hands and one foot. See if they can keep one hand flat and firm and practise keeping very still. Prompt them by asking: *What shape can you make with your free leg?* (Tuck it in, stretch out and so on.) Encourage them this time to take one hand away and make a still shape on one hand and both feet. Remind them to keep very still.

Let everyone choose their favourite balances to practise and refine. Encourage the children to practise these in different parts of the hall and to travel between their balances by sliding on their fronts or backs or moving on all fours.

Apparatus work

20 mins Remind the groups how to get out their apparatus and where to put it. (See pages 48–50, 154 and 160). When the apparatus has been set up, ask each group to point to the next pieces of apparatus they are to work on and to walk, when you tell them, to that apparatus and to sit in a space ready to begin.

Ask the children to practise making still shapes on different parts of their new apparatus. Encourage them to choose a space to start and to practise balancing, always looking for spaces. Remind them to use small steps, hops or small bunny-jump actions to travel between and around different parts of the apparatus.

Tell the children to balance on large parts of their body first, then move to another part of their apparatus and balance again. Repeat, seeing if they can balance on a smaller part or parts.

Encourage them to really stretch to make large, still shapes on different parts of their apparatus (holding, hanging or resting on the apparatus).

Ask everyone to choose their favourite shapes to practise. Encourage good spacing and travelling between balances. Then ask them to move down from their apparatus in interesting ways.

Ask them to point and then move to the next apparatus and repeat their actions and balances.

To finish, ask the groups to point to the apparatus that they got out and to walk back to it, sitting by the first piece they are to put away. When all of the children are settled, ask them to put their apparatus away.

Cool-down

3 mins When the apparatus is away, ask the children to find a space and to practise lots of little hops on the spot. Encourage light landings.

Diagram 12

Ask them to slowly tiptoe around the hall in all directions, slowing to a stop, then stretching and relaxing.

Ask the children to stand on tiptoes and to stretch up with their hands above their heads (see diagram 12). Ask them to slowly sink down into a small ball, holding the curled shape for ten seconds before lying down to relax. Repeat the sequence.

Classroom review

Ask the children if they could balance on two hands and one foot. *Was it easy or hard to keep still? What could you do with your free leg?* (For example, tuck it in, stretch it out to the side or across the body.)

Assessing learning outcomes

Can the children take their weight on two hands and one foot? Are they beginning to clarify the shapes of their balances? Are they aware of others? Are they spacing well on the apparatus?

(35 mins) Can we make shapes using smaller parts of the body?

What you need and preparation

You will need apparatus accessible at the sides of the hall; an apparatus plan for six groups (see photocopiable page 154).

Remind the children beforehand about how to handle and use apparatus.

What to do

(4 mins) Warm-up

Ask the children to jog, then stride around the hall, always looking for spaces. Ask them to try another way of moving on their feet with big steps or jumps.

Encourage them to practise pigeon steps and then giant strides and to alternate between them.

Play 'Large and small' (see pages 67 and 70), with the children choosing their large or small steps or jumps and making large or small still shapes as instructed by you.

(10 mins) Floor work

Ask the children to show you some of their favourite still shapes and balances. Select some good examples of the use of large parts and large shapes to show and then ask them all to try some. Select a few children to demonstrate using large parts and *small* shapes. Draw attention to the differences in size then ask everyone to practise their favourites and some new ones.

Encourage the children to try using smaller parts of their body to make still shapes (such as knees and hands or knees and elbows).

Ask the children to try a still shape on a smaller part of their feet (toes or heels) with their feet wide apart or together. Encourage them to try more than one way. Ask them which is easier.

Now tell them to try a still shape on one foot. Encourage the use of arms to help them to keep still. Ask them to try large, wide shapes and then small, curled shapes.

(18 mins) Apparatus work

Remind the groups how to get out their apparatus and where to put it. When the apparatus is out, ask the children to make *large*, still shapes on large parts of their bodies or *small*, still shapes on large parts of their bodies.

Encourage them to vary the use of large parts of the bodies such as their back, side or other parts (knees, bottom, tummy, shoulders and so on). Encourage them to use different parts of their apparatus (for example underneath planks or bars; against pieces of apparatus; resting on the floor or mat; resting one part of their body on the apparatus and another part on floor).

Ask the children to find places where they can use smaller parts of the body to balance on (for example holding on with two hands and one foot).

Now let them choose two, then three, of their favourite still shapes which are on different parts of the apparatus. Ask them to show their shapes one after the other.

Afterwards, ask them to point and then move to the next apparatus and repeat the tasks.

To finish, ask the children in their groups to point to the apparatus that they set up and to walk back to it, then sit by the first piece they are to put away. When they are settled, ask them to put their apparatus away.

(3 mins) Cool-down

When the apparatus is all away safely, ask the children to skip on the spot and then in and out around the space as lightly as they can. Encourage them to slow down gradually and try a slow-motion skip.

Learning objectives
● Explore and practise using smaller parts of the body to balance on the floor and apparatus.
● Explore and practise shapes on bottom and shoulders and other small parts of the body.
● Explore and practise still shapes on two hands and one foot, and on one foot.

Lesson organisation
Brief classroom discussion; individual warm-up and floor work; apparatus work in six groups; individual cool-down; teacher-led classroom review.

Vocabulary
pigeon steps
skipping

Next, tell the children to stand on tiptoes and to stretch up with their hands above their heads, then slowly sink down into a small ball, holding a curled shape for ten seconds before lying down to relax. Repeat this stretch and curl sequence.

Classroom review
Ask the children which small parts of their body they used. Get them to describe to a partner two of the different balances they tried. What helped them to keep still?

Assessing learning outcomes
Are the children able to use smaller parts of their bodies? Can they distinguish between small and large parts? Can they distinguish between large and small shapes?

(35 mins) Can we link our balances?

Learning objectives
● Practise balancing on one foot, clarifying the shape of the non- weight-bearing leg.
● Explore a combination of small parts to balance on.
● Select, practise and refine several balances to incorporate into a sequence.
● Start to link balances together to form a sequence on the floor and apparatus.
● Constructively comment on a partner's linked balances.

Lesson organisation
Brief classroom discussion; individual warm-up; individual and paired floor work; apparatus work in six groups; individual cool-down; classroom review in pairs.

What you need and preparation
You will need apparatus and a plan for six groups (see photocopiable page 154).
Remind the children of the procedures for lifting and carrying apparatus.

What to do

(4 mins) Warm-up
Ask the children to walk then skip or gallop around the area, using all the spaces. Encourage the use of all directions. Encourage them to lift their knees high.
Play a non-elimination version of 'Simon says', using different travelling actions (such as jogging and hopping) and different size steps and jumps.

(8 mins) Floor work
Let the children practise some of their favourite still shapes using different parts of their bodies. Ask them to select some large and some small parts. Choose some children to illustrate good examples. Advise the children to think about using large and small parts.
Ask everyone to practise balancing on one foot. Help them to clarify the shape of the non-weight-bearing leg by asking for ideas (such as stretching it out in front or to the side; tucking it to the chest). Ask them to choose two to practise. Encourage them to use a combination of small parts of the body to balance on (knee and hands, bottom and one hand and so on).
When everyone has explored, tried and practised many still shapes, encourage the children to select and link two then three together with a travelling action in between. (For example, balance on two hands and one foot, bunny jump into a space, sit back and balance on shoulders.) Tell the children to practise this several times, beginning to think about starting and finishing positions.
Ask the children to form pairs. One partner should show the other their linked balances, then swap. Those watching should try to pick out the different-sized shapes, and think how they could help their partner to clarify the action.
Ask half the class to show their still shapes while the others watch to see if they can pick out the different-sized shapes. Repeat, with the other half performing.

(20 mins) Apparatus work
In their groups, ask the children to carefully put out their apparatus, one piece at a time. Ask them to move to the next part of the apparatus and space out ready to begin.
Tell them first to choose, practise and consolidate some different balances on different parts of their apparatus.

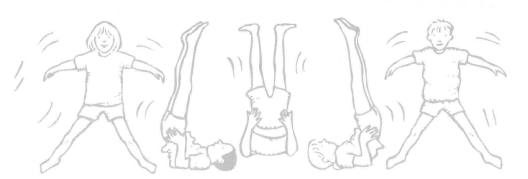

Watch them as they each practise and refine their choice by developing a sequence of balances on the apparatus with a travelling action in between (balance–travel–balance).

Ask half the groups to show their sequences while the other groups make comments on their spacing and balance. Swap over, then encourage them all to practise their sequence again, bearing in mind the comments of their classmates.

Next, instruct them to point and then move to their next apparatus and repeat the work they have just done.

To finish, ask them to point to the apparatus that they set up, walk back to it and sit by the first piece they are to put away. When they are settled, ask them to put their apparatus away.

③ Cool-down
mins Ask the children to skip on the spot, and then in and out around the space, as lightly as they can. Tell them to slow down gradually and to try a slow-motion skip.

Ask the children to stand on their tiptoes and to stretch up with their hands high above their heads. Instruct them to slowly sink down into a small ball and then lie down and stretch into a long, thin shape for ten seconds and then relax. Tell them to repeat this stretch–curl–stretch sequence to finish.

Classroom review
Ask the children to discuss with their partner what they thought was good about each other's performance – interesting shapes, kept very still and so on, and how they could improve next time – for example stretch a bit more, hold for the count of three.

Assessing learning outcomes
Were the children able to comment constructively on their partners' balances? Were they able to suggest ideas for improvement to their partner? Can they use a combination of small parts of the body to balance on?

⟨30 mins⟩ Can we improve our sequence of balances?

What you need and preparation
You will need apparatus accessible at the sides of the hall; an apparatus plan for six groups (see photocopiable page 154).

In the classroom, remind the children of the correct ways of handling apparatus.

What to do
④ Warm-up
mins Ask the children to walk then stride around the area, using all the spaces. Encourage small then much larger steps.

Play non-elimination 'Simon says', keeping the activity level high, and emphasising large and small steps and jumps.

⑥ Floor work
mins Ask the children to practise balancing on one foot, remembering some of the interesting shapes they made in the previous lesson.

Encourage the children to select some large and some small parts of their bodies to rest on. Ask them to choose a starting position and then practise linking the shapes together with a travelling action in between (for example holding the balance–travelling–holding the balance).

Vocabulary
skip
gallop
linking

Learning objective
Practise and refine a sequence on the floor and apparatus.

Lesson organisation
Brief classroom discussion; individual warm-up and floor work; six groups to handle and use apparatus; individual cool-down; teacher-led classroom review.

Balancing and making shapes

Vocabulary
stride
sequence
smooth

(18 mins) Apparatus work

In groups, ask the children to carefully put out their apparatus, one piece at a time. Ask them to move to the next part of the apparatus and space out ready to begin.

See if they can remember some of the various balances, and ask them to practise them on different parts of their apparatus.

Ask them to practise joining them together to make a sequence of movements on the floor and/or on the apparatus (balance–travel–balance).

Encourage them to repeat their sequence, trying to make the joins between the movements as smooth as they can. Tell the groups to rotate to a new apparatus and repeat their sequences.

Ask them to put their own apparatus away carefully at the end of the session.

(2 mins) Cool-down

Ask the children to move around the hall carefully on all fours (for example 'walking' on all fours or bunny jumping).

Then ask them to shake their bodies all over and then to lie down and relax and to think about the sequences they have just made.

Classroom review

Ask the children if they can remember their sequence and describe it to a partner.

Assessing learning outcomes

Are the children able to perform a variety of balances using both the floor and the apparatus? Are they able to repeat and refine a sequence of linked actions? Are they able to share the space fairly and safely with others?

Pushing and pulling – travelling and balancing

The focus for this series of lessons is developing children's experience of travelling (particularly sliding and jumping) and balancing. The sessions will raise children's awareness of the specific actions of pushing and pulling, while developing their movement vocabulary and their use of different parts of the body. It is particularly appropriate to use this theme to link with forces and motion in science (Sc4 2a–c).

The unit is divided into six sessions, allowing 30–40 minutes of activity per session. Each session will involve both floor and apparatus work, but ideas can be modified to suit individual school contexts. The class could be divided into six groups to ensure good spacing and fair turns on each group of apparatus (see the suggested apparatus plan on photocopiable page 155).

It is presumed that children will have had experience of different ways of travelling on different parts of the body and that their landings are becoming more controlled. Because many of the actions involve sliding on the body, it is important that the floor and the apparatus are clean and smooth and in good condition.

Cross-curricular links with science

Discussions in the classroom will have introduced children to forces that can make things move. This theme will enhance children's understanding of pushing and pulling forces by encouraging them to explore different ways that pushes and pulls can be used to move or hold the body. Through contexts in PE which are familiar, through trying out and investigating with their own bodies and through describing what they have done, children will develop a greater understanding of these forces.

They will use their muscles to push – to hold a still shape; to pull – to hold a still shape. The lessons emphasise muscles pulling and pushing (working hard) to hold still positions or balances.

Using muscles to push up into the air – to jump – demonstrates using muscles like springs to push the body upwards. Children will also become aware of gravity bringing them down and of forces being absorbed on landing (resilience).

As they practise, children will become more aware of the ways in which they use their muscles to push, pull, jump, travel and climb.

UNIT 3: Pushing and pulling – travelling and balancing

Enquiry questions	Learning objectives	Teaching activities	Learning outcomes
What methods of pushing are there?	● Practise ways of absorbing the effects of gravity on landing. ● Explore ways of pushing with the legs and arms to assist jumping. ● Try ways of pushing with the arms to make still shapes on all fours. ● Practise ways of pushing on the floor and benches.	Warm-up: practising little bounces on the spot and in all directions; practising ways of travelling on the feet. Floor work: practising squashy landings using arms to jump; using hands and feet to make still shapes; practising lying down and pushing up into shapes; trying ways of travelling on hands and feet; trying bunny jumps, pushing with hands. Apparatus work: in six groups: trying pushing actions away from, along and around the bench; using hands and feet to make still shapes partly on bench, partly on floor; practising bunny jumps on bench and floor; practising favourite pushing actions. Cool-down: lying down and relaxing, making the body go floppy then tight.	Children: ● control their landings ● push with their legs and swing their arms to help them jump ● understand the idea of pushing with their legs or pushing with their hands
Can we find more ways of pushing?	● Practise ways of jumping and landing, pushing forwards and upwards. ● Explore ways of pushing with the legs and arms to travel on the body, on the floor and on the apparatus. ● Select and practise ways of pushing and show them to a partner.	Warm-up: running on the spot and around the space, changing direction; playing 'Statue stops'. Floor work: making big strides and little jumps, practising jumping and landing; trying different shapes in the air; practising ways of moving on the body using legs and arms to push; practising still shapes and showing partner pushing actions. Apparatus work: in six groups: trying pushing actions away from, along and around the benches; practising jumping and landing. Cool-down: lying down, relaxing, stretching.	● understand how to push with their legs and arms
Can we push up, forwards and along, using hands and feet?	● Practise travelling on the feet, pushing with legs. ● Practise using hands to push on the floor. ● Practise using feet to push on the floor and apparatus. ● Explore ways of pushing with the legs and arms to assist jumping. ● Refine the shapes of jumps.	Warm-up: running on the spot, lifting knees and heels up; playing 'Statue stops'. Floor work: running with lengthening stride; practising jumping and landing; moving on the body, pushing with legs and showing to a partner. Apparatus work: trying different pushing actions around the apparatus; selecting and practising two different pushing actions. Cool-down: with hands flat on the floor, jumping feet forwards and backwards; relaxing.	● use their hands and feet to push ● space well on the apparatus ● improve their jumping
Can we pull with our arms?	● Practise pushing with arms to bunny jump and with the legs to cat spring. ● Try pulling actions. ● Try ways of pulling with the arms to make still shapes on apparatus.	Warm-up: skipping on the spot and around the space, gradually lifting feet higher; using skipping to play 'Traffic light statues'. Floor work: practising pushing actions in different directions; trying out cat springs; trying ways of pulling along. Apparatus work: practising different still shapes; holding on to or pulling away from the apparatus to make still shapes; pulling along parts of the apparatus. Cool-down: jumping on the spot, gradually getting lower until sitting; lying and relaxing.	● understand and demonstrate pulling actions

Enquiry questions	Learning objectives	Teaching activities	Learning outcomes
Can we improve our pushing and pulling actions?	● Practise ways of absorbing the effects of gravity on landing (hop). ● Practise special pushing and pulling actions to put into a sequence. ● Practise ways of pulling the body on the apparatus and pulling to make shapes. ● Try ways of pushing and pulling and start linking them together on the floor and apparatus.	Warm-up: hopping on the spot and around the space. Floor work: practising different ways of pulling using different parts of the body; clarifying shapes; practising pushing up into still shapes on hands and feet; practising jumps, lowering down onto backs or fronts to push or pull; practising two or three pushing or pulling movements and linking together. Apparatus work: practising pushing and pulling to move from one part of the apparatus to another; trying ways of jumping to get on and off apparatus; choosing favourite pushing and pulling actions and linking together. Cool-down: making slow-motion jumps; tucking and stretching.	● select appropriate pushing and pulling actions for their sequences ● demonstrate an awareness of others as they use the apparatus
Can we link pushing and pulling actions?	● Practise ways of absorbing the effects of gravity (landing one leg after the other). ● Explore ways of pushing with the arms to bunny jump in different directions. ● Select and practise ways of pushing and pulling to create a sequence on the floor and apparatus.	Warm-up: practising moving and then linking different ways of travelling on feet. Floor work: practising different jumps; practising pushing and pulling actions and linking together. Apparatus work: practising two pushing and two pulling actions and linking them together to make a sequence on the apparatus; watching and commenting on others' performances. Cool-down: in pairs, joining hands, pulling away from each other and standing up and sitting down.	● demonstrate their knowledge of pushing and pulling by linking their chosen actions into a sequence ● describe their pushing and pulling actions.

Cross-curricular links
Science: gaining understanding and experience of pushing and pulling forces, absorbing forces, gravity.

Resources
Apparatus; photocopiable pages 155 and 160; paper; drawing materials.

Pushing and pulling – travelling and balancing

(35 mins) What methods of pushing are there?

Learning objectives
● Practise ways of absorbing the effects of gravity on landing.
● Explore ways of pushing with the legs and arms to assist jumping.
● Try ways of pushing with the arms to make still shapes on all fours.
● Practise ways of pushing on the floor and benches.

Lesson organisation
Brief classroom discussion classroom; individual warm-up and floor work; apparatus practice in six groups; individual cool-down; teacher-led classroom review.

Vocabulary
pushing
gravity
absorbing forces
energy
squashy
resilient landings

What you need and preparation
You will need one bench or box-top for each of six groups (approximately five children per group).

In the classroom beforehand, discuss with the children the special requirements for getting to the hall and doing gymnastics (see Apparatus on page 48 of the chapter introduction).

What to do

(5 mins) Warm-up
Ensure children are well spaced to start the warm-up. Ask them to try little bounces on the spot and encourage quiet, resilient, squashy landings, bending hips, knees and ankles.

Start with the toes hardly leaving the floor, then gradually encourage the children to lift their feet a little higher off the ground.

Ask them to try the little bounces and jumps on the spot, then forwards and backwards and then in another direction (side to side or diagonally). Observe the responses and suggest everyone tries two different ways.

Encourage them to make a pattern of jumps as lightly as they can and to repeat them. This will raise the pulse and help them to remember a simple sequence of jumps.

Practise different ways of travelling on the feet – hopping, jumping, jogging, while moving around the hall looking for spaces.

(12 mins) Floor work
In their own space again, encourage the children to practise a higher jump with a squashy landing (to absorb the forces of gravity).

Ask the children to explore ways of pushing with the legs (like a spring) and encourage the children to use their arms to assist jumping (see Diagram 13). For children who need extra challenges, encourage them to make different shapes in the air.

Ask the class to use their hands and feet to make a still shape. Emphasise strong, straight arms and flat hands to support the body. Encourage them to make other shapes with their hands and feet on the floor, for example press-up or front support position, hands and feet wide apart, low, near the ground, with tummy uppermost (see Diagram 14) or back uppermost.

Diagram 13

Diagram 14

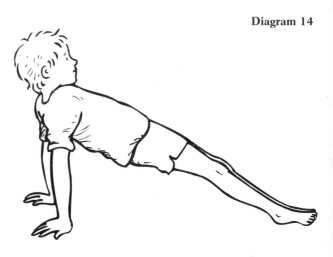

**Pushing and pulling
– travelling and
balancing**

Now tell them to lie down and push up into the shape they just practised. Encourage keeping body shape and tension and help the children to refine their shapes.

Ask them to try a way of travelling on hands and feet, pushing with the hands to move along. Choose individual children to demonstrate two or three ways to the rest of the class. Then ask everyone to try one of the ways they have seen or a new way of their own.

Select a child trying a bunny jump or ask a child to demonstrate this action to introduce pushing with hands (both hands shoulder-width apart, arms straight, knees tucked and together, then both feet lifted together off the ground).

Practise bunny-jump actions together, emphasising flat hands, straight arms and light landings.

Apparatus work

15 mins With the children in six groups, ask each group to get out and set up one bench or box-top.

Ask the children to try out some of the pushing actions they have been trying this lesson, towards, away from, along, over or around the bench. Insist on looking for spaces and keeping moving.

Tell everyone to use their hands and their feet to make a still shape with part of them on the bench and part of them on the floor (see Diagram 15). Look for good examples to use to suggest ideas to other children.

Ask everyone to try a bunny jump to move along the bench or along the floor. Then encourage them to practise the bunny jump and emphasise pushing with hands along the bench, over the bench or around the bench (see Diagram 16). Ask the children if they can feel how strong their arms are to take the weight of their bodies.

Ask the children to have a go at a different way of travelling on their hands and feet, pushing with their hands. Choose children to illustrate two or three ways.

Tell everyone to select and practise their favourite pushing actions. Then ask the groups to put their apparatus away carefully.

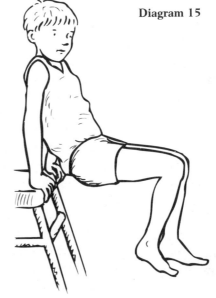

Diagram 15

Diagram 16

Cool-down

3 mins Ask the children to lie down and relax and make the body go all floppy. Tell them to pull all the muscles tight and then relax again. Ask them to tense and relax once more before getting ready to return to the classroom.

Classroom review

Encourage the children to describe some of the actions they tried, for example, pushing jump, pushing with their hands to make a shape. Ask: *What did you notice when you tried the bunny jump? What did you notice when you tried to travel along the bench?*

Assessing learning outcomes

Are all the children controlling their landings? Are they pushing with their legs and swinging their arms to help them jump? Do they all understand the idea of pushing with their legs and pushing with their hands?

**Pushing and pulling
– travelling and
balancing**

35 mins Can we find more ways of pushing?

Learning objectives
● Practise ways of jumping and landing, pushing forwards and upwards.
● Explore ways of pushing with the legs and arms to travel on the body, on the floor and on the apparatus.
● Select and practise ways of pushing and show them to a partner.

Lesson organisation
Brief classroom discussion; individual warm-up; individual and paired floor work; apparatus work in six groups; individual cool-down; teacher-led classroom review.

Vocabulary
pushing
gravity
absorbing forces
energy
squashy
resilient landings

What you need and preparation
You will need apparatus and a plan for six groups (see photocopiable page 155).

Discuss in the classroom the particular requirements for getting out and using apparatus (see page 48 and photocopiable page 160).

What to do

5 mins Warm-up
Ask the children to try little running steps on the spot, lightly lifting the feet and pointing the toes, and then moving around the hall. Check their spacing and encourage small steps and free movement with lots of changes of direction. Play a non-elimination game of 'Statue stops', telling the children to stop still on your signal.

12 mins Floor work
Ask the class to try bigger strides. Ask what happens if they want to make *much* bigger strides. Advise them to practise pushing with each leg in turn to increase their stride.

Now tell them to try little bounces on the spot, gradually getting lower and lower and then pushing more with the legs to get gradually higher.

Ask the children what different shapes they can make in the air, and then tell them to practise jumping and making a shape. (They could try star, tucked and long, thin shapes, for example.) Emphasise pushing with the legs and bending the hips, knees and ankles to absorb the forces of gravity on landing.

Ask them to lie down. This could be on their backs, sides or fronts. Ask them what they must remember to do before they move. (Look for spaces.) Tell them to move on that part of their body to another space. Help them to become aware of which part of the body is touching the floor and then, more importantly, which part they are using most to move themselves along. Say: *Are you using your legs or your arms?*

Use a few examples for demonstration and then encourage everyone to try one of these ideas or a new way of their own. It could be that two children are on their backs but are pushing themselves along in a different way, for example using two feet, only one foot or just hands. Ask everyone: *Are you using two feet or one? What happens if you only push with one foot?*

Diagram 17

In pairs, ask the children to show each other the ways of pushing they had chosen and then say something they liked about their partner's actions.

15 mins Apparatus work
Refer to the apparatus section in the chapter introduction (pages 48–50) and the apparatus plan on photocopiable page 155. In their six groups, show the children how to get out their allocated apparatus and where to put it. Ask them to space out and to move around their apparatus, keeping in spaces.

Encourage them to try out some of the pushing actions they have performed previously: towards, away from, along, over

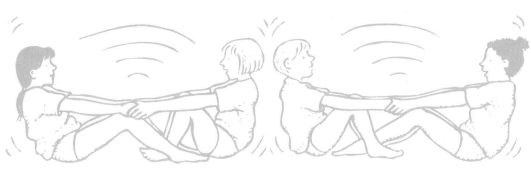

or around their group's apparatus. Remind them to try using their hands to push and then try using their legs to push. Continue to prompt the children to look for spaces and keep moving.

Ask the children to find places where they can push with their hands and hold a still shape on different parts of the apparatus (see Diagrams 17 and 18). Look for children to demonstrate different possibilities, to suggest ideas or to challenge other children.

Ask all the children to use lower parts of their apparatus, from where they can practise jumping and landing. Then let them select and practise their favourite interesting pushing actions.

To finish, ask the groups to put their apparatus away carefully.

3 mins Cool-down
Ask the children to lie down and relax and make their bodies go all floppy. Tell them to stretch their arms and legs as wide as possible and relax again. Repeat this stretch–relax sequence several times.

Diagram 18

Classroom review

Ask the children to describe some of the actions they tried in the lesson, for example a pushing jump, pushing with hands or feet as they moved on their bodies. Ask: *Which did you like trying best – pushing with the hands or the feet or using both? What happened when you only used one hand or foot?*

Assessing learning outcomes

Are the children understanding pushing with their legs and arms?

35 mins Can we push up, forwards and along using hands and feet?

What you need and preparation

You will need apparatus and a plan for six groups (see photocopiable page 155).

In the classroom, discuss with the children the special requirements for setting up and using apparatus (see pages 48–50 of the chapter introduction and photocopiable page 160).

What to do

5 mins Warm-up
Ask the children to try little running steps on the spot, gradually lifting the knees and then moving around the hall. Let them try this again but this time with their heels up behind them. Play 'Statue stops', reminding the children to stop *still* on the signal *Stop*. Check the children's spacing and encourage small steps and free movement with lots of changes of direction.

10 mins Floor work
Ask the children to practise these running steps, but sometimes pushing upwards with their legs. Then ask them to try pushing forwards with their legs to lengthen their stride. Follow on by experimenting with the different ways of pushing with the legs and arms to assist jumping. Check that they are landing safely.

Learning objectives
● Practise travelling on feet, pushing with legs.
● Practise using hands to push on the floor and the apparatus.
● Practise using feet to push on the floor and apparatus.
● Explore ways of pushing with the legs and arms to assist jumping.
● Refine the shapes of jumps.

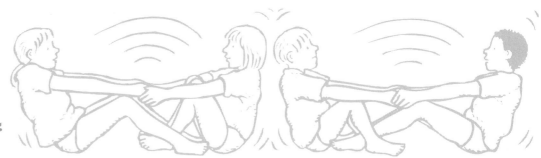

Pushing and pulling – travelling and balancing

Ask the children to remember the shapes they made in the air when they jumped and to choose and practise some. Emphasise pushing with the legs and bending the knees to absorb the forces on landing.

Ask the children to position themselves down on the floor. This could be on their backs, sides or fronts or on smaller parts such as shoulders. Encourage them to try a different part of their body this time. Tell them to move on that part of their body to another space, pushing with their legs. Ask: *How did you find that? How easy or difficult was it?*

Use a few of the children's examples for demonstration and then encourage all the children to try a new way of their own. Ask them: *How is it different from your last way of moving?*

Before they move on to the apparatus, organise the children into pairs and ask them to show each other the movements they have chosen and suggest how they could be improved.

(18 mins) Apparatus work

In their six groups, ask the children to get out their allocated apparatus, and then to move to the apparatus they are to work on. (See page 49 for ways of rotating the groups.)

Ask the children to use all parts of the apparatus, looking for spaces. Then ask them to try some of the pushing actions they have tried so far: towards, away from, along, over or around their group's apparatus. Make sure they are looking for spaces and keeping moving.

Ask the class to use their bodies to push themselves along, under or around parts of the apparatus.

Let the children select and practise examples of using their hands to push, then select and practise examples of using their legs to push. Ask a few children to demonstrate some of the different possibilities, to suggest ideas to or challenge other children. Encourage them to keep good control of their actions.

Ask everyone to practise some more still shapes. Then ask them to point and move to the next apparatus and repeat the tasks.

To finish, ask the groups to return to the apparatus they got out and to put it away carefully.

(2 mins) Cool-down

Ask the children, placing their hands flat on the floor, to push with their arms straight and jump their feet forwards and backwards. Tell them to finish in the front support position and lower their bodies slowly to the ground. Ask everyone to relax and let their bodies go floppy.

Classroom review
Briefly discuss the lesson. Ask the children: *How did you improve your actions today? What did you enjoy performing the most?*

Assessing learning outcomes
Are the children using their hands and their feet to push? Are they spacing well on the apparatus? Has their jumping improved?

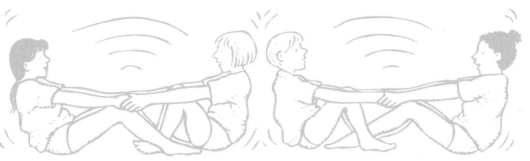

(35 mins) Can we pull with our arms?

What you need and preparation

You will need apparatus and an apparatus plan for six groups (see photocopiable page 155).

Discuss with children in the classroom the special requirements for getting out and using apparatus (see Apparatus on pages 48–50 and the diagrams on photocopiable page 160).

What to do

(5 mins) Warm-up

Ask the children to skip on the spot and then around the hall. Then encourage them to use stronger pushes to skip, lifting their feet higher off the ground.

Use skipping to play a traffic-light statues game (non-elimination). Instructions could be, for example:

- Amber – skip on the spot.
- Green – skip around the hall.
- Red – stop still.

(10 mins) Floor work

Ask the children to practise pushing with their hands to make still shapes (see Diagram 19).

Then ask everyone to practise some other pushing actions that they have done in previous lessons. Remind them how to do a bunny jump if necessary. Emphasise ways of pushing with the arms to bunny jump and encourage movement in different directions.

Diagram 19

Ask them to try a movement that is similar to a bunny jump but that travels further and pushes with the legs (like a pounce) – a cat spring. Go through the movement with them: from a crouch position, reach hands forward just a few inches from the ground; push with legs, hands flat, arms absorbing the weight, then both legs catching up to return to a crouch position.

After a few minutes practising cat springs, let the children lie down on their backs or fronts and try to pull themselves along the floor. Ask them: *What is the difference between a pushing and a pulling action?* Encourage them to reach and pull with the arms and then try out different pulling actions. Use some of the children's ideas to demonstrate and to suggest actions to others. Point out their movements: *Watch how they are using their arms to pull themselves along. What parts of the body are they resting on?*

Learning objectives
- Practise pushing with arms to bunny jump and with legs to cat spring.
- Try pulling actions.
- Try pulling with the arms to make still shapes on apparatus.

Lesson organisation
Brief classroom discussion; individual warm-up and floor work; apparatus practice in six groups; individual cool-down; classroom review in pairs.

Vocabulary
pull
cat spring
bunny jump
pounce
push
absorb weight

**Pushing and pulling
– travelling and
balancing**

18 **Apparatus work**
mins Refer to the apparatus section of the chapter introduction and the apparatus plan on photocopiable page 155. In their six groups, ask the children to get out and set up their allocated apparatus and to move to their next arrangement.

Ask the children to find places on the apparatus where they can make still shapes. Encourage good spacing and use of all parts of the apparatus, including the floor. This could involve sitting, lying, hanging or holding (see Diagram 20).

Diagram 20

Ask the children to find different places where they can hold on to or pull away from a piece of apparatus and make a still shape. Emphasise stillness, holding the shape for the count of three and then moving to another part of the apparatus to make another shape that involves pulling away from the apparatus.

Tell everyone to find places where they can hold under a piece of apparatus and make a still shape (see Diagram 21). Ask them: *Can you feel your arms pulling?*

Diagram 21

Now ask the children to find parts of their apparatus where they can pull themselves along. Let them select and practise different ways of pulling on different parts of the apparatus. Prompt them with questions such as *Where are the best places for pulling? Can you use any other parts of the apparatus?*

Then ask the children to point and then move to the next apparatus and repeat the above tasks.

To finish, ask the groups to put their own apparatus away carefully.

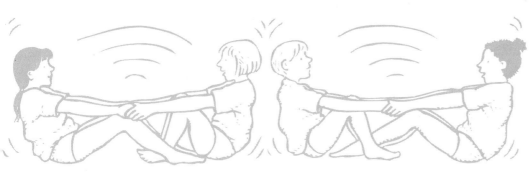

**Pushing and pulling
– travelling and
balancing**

2
mins **Cool-down**
Ask the children to find a space and jump on the spot, slowly getting lower and lower until they can sit back and lie down.

Tell them to stretch out in a long, thin shape and relax, and then to try it again.

Classroom review

Ask the children to think of three different ways they used pulling actions on the apparatus, and describe them to a partner. Encourage their discussion by asking questions like:
- Which ways did you try to pull yourselves along the floor?
- Which still shapes did you use to pull away from the apparatus?
- Which parts of the apparatus did you use?

Assessing learning outcomes

Do the children understand and can they demonstrate pulling actions?

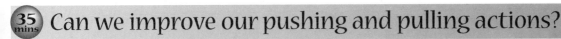

35
mins # Can we improve our pushing and pulling actions?

What you need and preparation

You will need apparatus and a plan for six groups (see photocopiable page 155).

Beforehand, in the classroom, remind the children of the special requirements for getting out apparatus (see Apparatus on pages 48–50 and photocopiable page 160).

What to do

4
mins **Warm-up**
Ask the children to hop on the spot (changing legs after a short while) and then to hop around the hall. Encourage a stronger hop with the legs and use of the arms to hop higher and over a greater distance.

Ask them to choose and practise their own way of moving around the space.

15
mins **Floor work**
Ask the children to choose their favourite ways of pulling themselves along. Encourage them to use different parts of the body. Ask them to clarify what shape they are making with their legs. (This could be legs together, legs apart or legs tucked and will help them to refine the shape of the actions.) Check that they are using good pulling actions.

Ask them if they can remember the still shapes on hands and feet that they have tried in previous sessions. Tell them to think carefully to choose one and encourage them to practise pushing up into it slowly.

Now tell them to practise pushing up into a jump and then lowering themselves onto their backs or fronts to push or pull themselves along. They could then turn over and push themselves up into one of the still shapes on hands and feet that they have just practised.

Finally, before moving on to work on the apparatus, let everyone select and try two, then three, different ways of pushing and pulling: some still shapes, some moving. When the children have chosen and practised them, ask them to decide which one they want to start with and then practise them all, one after the other. Remind them to think carefully about how the movements can be linked together.

Ask the children if they have used different parts of their bodies and have included at least one push and pull. Are they using all the space? Ask them to try their linked actions again, thinking how smoothly they can join them together.

Learning objectives
- Practise ways of absorbing the effects of gravity on landing on one leg.
- Practise special pushing and pulling actions to put into a sequence.
- Practise ways of pulling the body on the apparatus and pulling to make still shapes.
- Further develop awareness of the use of space and others.
- Try ways of pushing and pulling and start linking them together on the floor and apparatus.

Lesson organisation
Brief classroom discussion; individual warm-up and floor work and apparatus practice in six groups; individual cool-down; classroom review in pairs.

Pushing and pulling – travelling and balancing

Vocabulary
pushing
pulling
sequence
linking actions

18 mins Apparatus work

Referring to the handling apparatus notes and apparatus plan, ask the children in their groups to get out their allocated apparatus. When it is ready, ask them to move to their next apparatus.

Ask the children to find different ways of pushing or pulling themselves along, moving from one part of the apparatus to another. Ask them to look carefully where they are going and to use the spaces on the apparatus.

Encourage them to find places where they can jump to get on or off the apparatus – using hands or feet. For example, onto or off from the benches, planks or flat platforms.

Let everyone choose their favourite pushing and pulling actions and practise them. See if they can start linking them together in the way that they did during the floor work.

Encourage them to think carefully about where they want to start (check their spacing) and to plan the pathway to get them to where they want to perform their next pulling or pushing action.

Tell the groups to move to the next apparatus and repeat the tasks, then ask them to put their apparatus away carefully.

3 mins Cool-down

Ask the children to perform slow-motion jumps, sinking down to the ground, tucking up small and then stretching out.

Classroom review

Ask the children to think about the different pushing and pulling actions that they chose or could choose to link together to make a sequence. Tell them to remember them for next week. Encourage them to tell a partner what they want to try to improve their actions next time.

Assessing learning outcomes

Are the children selecting appropriate pushing and pulling actions for their sequences? Are they demonstrating an awareness of others as they use the apparatus?

35 mins Can we link pushing and pulling actions?

Learning objectives
● Practise ways of absorbing the effects of gravity landing one foot after the other (leap).
● Refine chosen pushing and pulling actions.
● Improve ways of pushing and pulling to develop a sequence of linked actions on the floor and the apparatus.

What you need and preparation

You will need: apparatus and an apparatus plan for six groups (see photocopiable page 155); paper and drawing materials.

Remind the children in the classroom the special requirements for getting out apparatus (see the notes on handling and using apparatus on pages 48 and 160).

What to do

5 mins Warm-up

Ask the children to choose one way of moving around the hall on their feet (hop, jump, jog, stride, skip, and so on). Tell them to keep moving and changing direction, always looking for spaces. Ask them to try another way of moving on their feet and to change smoothly from one to the other after about eight to ten steps or jumps. For example, leaping then hopping; jumping then striding.

10 mins Floor work

Talk about all the different types of jumps that the children have tried over the past few sessions (star jump, leap, hop, bunny jump, cat spring and so on) and ask them to practise their favourites. Encourage them to emphasise pushing forwards, upwards or backwards as they practise and refine two different ways.

Look out for more practise that may be needed on one type of jump, and then suggest practising that jump (for example cat spring – pushing forwards; bunny jump – moving sideways or backwards). Stress to the children the importance of looking before they move and moving into spaces.

See if they can remember the pushing and pulling actions they chose last time and ask them to practise linking them together. Encourage two pushing and two pulling actions (some still, some moving) and then help them to focus on their starting and finishing positions.

17 mins Apparatus work

In their six groups, ask the children to get out their allocated apparatus and to move to the next arrangement they are to work on.

Ask everyone to remember and practise their favourite two pushing and two pulling actions from the last lesson. Ask them to practise ways of linking them together to make a sequence on the apparatus.

Watch half the groups in turn perform their linked sequences showing pushing and pulling actions. Ask the half watching to name and describe the pushing and pulling actions that they notice and think are interesting or done well. Are they using their hands and their feet and their bodies? Which parts of the apparatus are they using? Then ask the groups to swap, with the first half of the class now the audience.

To finish, ask all the groups to rotate to their next apparatus and repeat the tasks before putting their own apparatus away.

3 mins Cool-down

Ask the children to sit in pairs, facing each other with their knees bent and their feet nearly touching each other flat on the floor. Ask them to join hands and straighten their arms, pulling away from each other. Tell them to keep pulling back from each other, holding each other's hands firmly (see Diagram 22), and to try to stand up and then to sit down again.

Then ask them to separate and move away from their partners and let their whole bodies relax.

Diagram 22

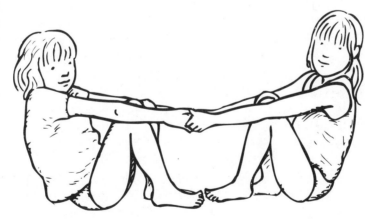

Classroom review
Ask the children to draw their favourite pushing and pulling actions.

Assessing learning outcomes
Can the children demonstrate their knowledge of pushing and pulling by linking their chosen actions into a sequence? Can they describe their pushing and pulling actions?

Lesson organisation
Brief classroom discussion; individual warm-up and floor work; apparatus practice in six groups; cool-down in pairs; teacher-led classroom review.

Vocabulary
practise
improve
refine
quality

Games

The enthusiasm and interest shown in this aspect of physical education makes it an ideal medium to provide a whole variety of experiences from which children may learn not just about how to perform games skills, but also about making choices and judgements, taking it in turns and co-operating with others.

Young children will have had a wide range of experiences when they start school, so enabling all of them to make progress, challenging some and encouraging others, is not an easy task. The units in this chapter aim to provide a basis for developing confidence and competence whatever the children's ability. It is important in the early stages of games playing that children have as much 'hands on' experience as possible – plenty of opportunities to handle and experiment individually with a wide variety of objects (balls, hoops, bats and so on) of different size, shape, texture and colour. Free play, however, does not automatically help children to learn new skills, to develop competence or raise awareness of what they are doing, so they often need to be guided towards new actions or activities. The process of learning to manipulate and control equipment takes practise as does making judgements and developing an awareness of speed, distance and direction. In each of the lessons therefore, there is a blend of guided or specified activity with other opportunities for choice or inventiveness. Large-group games activities or scaled-down versions of adult games are inappropriate for young children, so the emphasis is on situations where they are active and involved in manipulating, grasping, releasing, handling, holding, balancing, striking, receiving, retrieving, aiming and passing equipment.

The activities suggested seek to promote the development of positive attitudes, as well as stimulating experiences that encourage children to use their initiative, to help them to think about what they are doing, to plan, evaluate and learn about the effects of exercise on their bodies.

The warm-up activities encourage children to engage in a variety of fun games situations which provide opportunities to prepare the body for exercise and to develop a variety of skills. (A selection of warm-up games is provided on photocopiable pages 156–9.) The gradual build up to vigorous activity to raise the pulse and breathing rate and to get the muscles warm is intended to be fun and, although challenge is necessary, it is important that the games are non-elimination so that all the children receive the benefit of all of the activity. Included are activities that encourage children to try out and practise:

- listening and responding to instructions
- different actions (walking, jogging, leaping, hopping)
- different speeds
- moving in different directions safely and with agility
- skills of stopping and starting and changing direction
- developing an awareness of space, of others and of apparatus.

Opportunities are then given for them to try out, practise and modify their skills, sometimes with quite specific guidance and sometimes enabling them to take control, make choices and decisions and learn to co-operate and share the space and equipment. These are followed by situations in which children are able to plan and devise or play games with a partner.

Cool-down activities help to calm and settle the children before returning to the classroom.

To ensure progress and continued involvement it is important that the initial stages of games playing are positive, satisfying and yet challenging experiences.

These lessons should ideally be taken outside wherever possible so that children will have the opportunity for vigorous activity in a large space in the fresh air.

Colour-coded equipment is recommended for ease of organisation and to enable and encourage children to develop a sense of responsibility for taking out and using, checking and putting away the equipment.

It would be a good idea to have four regular colour groups with a list of names on the classroom wall for ease of reference. Each group can be made responsible for one basket of equipment –

collecting it from the PE cupboard, carrying and placing it in the corners of the space to be used. This has a number of advantages:
- The playing area is defined.
- Children have a feeling of responsibility for the equipment.
- The equipment is dispersed for easier collection (minimising congestion).
- The time spent for collecting and returning the equipment is minimised.
- Tidying and checking the equipment at the end of each session is made easier.
- Children are involved in counting, colour-coding, looking after and checking their own equipment and baskets.
- The equipment will be ready for the next class.

Exploring rings and hoops
This unit provides opportunities to guide children as they explore and practise using rubber rings (quoits) and hoops in a variety of ways, increasing their vocabulary of ideas and actions. Many of the activities can be modified for use with other apparatus.

Jumping, skipping and bouncing
This unit combines practise of a selection of bouncing, jumping and skipping skills that challenge children individually and in pairs and help them to participate in practical mathematical activities.

Developing bat and ball skills
This unit seeks to introduce, consolidate and develop skills using a bat and a ball.

Exploring rings and hoops

This unit will help children to explore and familiarise themselves with small apparatus, particularly rubber rings (quoits) and hoops. It is assumed that children will already have had some familiarisation with beanbags and large and small balls in a context that allows for individual exploration and practise.

The aim is for as much 'hands on' experience and practise as possible, and therefore sufficient equipment should be available for one piece each.

A developing awareness of breathing rate, leading to an understanding of how the body works, is also part of the focus for these sessions.

UNIT: Exploring rings and hoops

Enquiry questions	Learning objectives	Teaching activities	Learning outcomes
Can we use rubber rings?	● Become familiar with handling rubber rings – carrying, spinning, passing from hand to hand. ● Explore the changes that occur in breathing rate as a result of vigorous activity. ● Practise individually with selected pieces of equipment.	Warm-up: notice breathing before activity; jogging on the spot and around the space; playing 'Two, one, other'; notice breathing after activity. Development: passing a ring from hand to hand around different parts of the body; walking around a ring in different ways; playing the car game; jumping over the ring in different directions; spinning the ring on the floor, pouncing to stop it, adding an action; practising with the ring, setting personal challenges. Games: choosing, playing and practising with one piece of equipment. Cool-down: walking while balancing a ring on the head, bending down to touch the floor; passing the ring around the body.	Children: ● sustain vigorous activity ● manipulate and handle the rings well
Can we try more ways of using the rings?	● Make good use of space ● Practise putting down, picking up and carrying rings in different ways. ● Practise different ways of passing rings individually and in pairs, and make up a game with a partner.	Warm-up: jogging on the spot and around the space; playing the car game and 'Stop and go'. Development: jogging away from and returning to a ring; practising ways of using rings; passing the ring to a partner using different positions. Games: counting passes in pairs; making up a game of passing in pairs; practising individually with one piece of equipment. Cool-down: walking while balancing a ring on the head; playing 'Help each other'; stretching the ring in the air and passing it around the body.	● make good use of space ● show an awareness of others ● handle the rings with confidence and control
What ways of passing the ring can we try?	● Practise carrying, putting down, picking up, rolling and catching a ring. ● Practise different ways of passing a ring in pairs. ● Make up a game of passing in pairs.	Warm-up: jogging on the spot and around the space; playing 'Two, one, other' and 'Stop and go'. Development: stepping over the ring in different directions; practising spinning the ring; rolling the ring and walking alongside it; throwing the ring into the air and catching it; rolling the ring to a partner. Games: making up a game of rolling with a partner; practising passing the ring to a partner in different ways; making up a game of passing without dropping the ring; practising individually with one piece of equipment. Cool-down: playing 'Help each other'; stretching with the ring high; passing the ring around the body.	● make good use of space ● show an awareness of others ● roll and pass the ring
Can we use hoops?	● Practise jumping patterns in and out of a hoop. ● Try different ways of turning a hoop around the body. ● Try to intercept a partner as they run from one side of the playground to another.	Warm-up: jogging in different directions; standing in a hoop and practising lifting it over the head and lowering it down; jogging around the hoops. Development: lifting the hoop over the head and putting it down quickly; jumping in and out of the hoop in different ways and making a pattern of jumps; practising with the hoop; trying to hula-hoop. Games: practising individually with one piece of equipment; playing 'Farmer, may we cross your river?' Cool-down: jogging slowly in different directions.	● repeat jumping patterns in their hoops ● manage the hula-hoop

UNIT: Exploring rings and hoops

Enquiry questions	Learning objectives	Teaching activities	Learning outcomes
Can we develop our actions with the hoop?	● Intercept a partner as they run from one side of the playground to another. ● Practise rolling and stopping a hoop individually and with a partner. ● Throw a beanbag into a hoop in different ways.	Warm-up: jogging on the spot and around the space, alternating speed; jogging and stopping in the hoop; playing 'Numbers'; playing 'Parts of the body'. Development: holding hoop upright and moving through it; rolling and collecting the hoop; rolling the hoop to a partner; practising throwing a beanbag underarm into a hoop, trying various ways. Games: practising individually with one piece of equipment; playing 'Farmer, may we cross your river?' Cool-down: playing 'Back to front'; jogging then walking; stretching to relax.	● roll and collect a hoop ● think of ways to get past their partners in the farmer game
Can we skip with a hoop?	● Practise the hula-hoop. ● Jump in and out of a hoop held near the ground by a partner. ● Practise skipping with a hoop. ● Roll a hoop in different ways. ● Be mindful when using hoops.	Warm-up: practising the hula-hoop; jogging around the hoops; playing 'Parts of the body'. Development: practising the hula-hoop; skipping in the hoop; rolling the hoop to a partner; rolling the hoop using backspin; holding the hoop low for a partner to jump into. Games: practising individually with one piece of equipment; playing 'Farmer, may we cross your river?' Cool-down: playing 'back to front'; jogging then walking; stretching to relax.	● skip with a hoop ● are mindful of others as they use their hoops.

Cross-curricular links
Science: gaining understanding of breathing and how the human body works.
PSHE: learning to share; working as a team.

Resources
Colour-coded baskets; enough rings, beanbags, various-sized balls, hoops for one each; space outside in the fresh air whenever possible; photocopiable pages 156 and 157.

(30 mins) Can we use rubber rings?

What you need and preparation

You will need: colour-coded baskets containing rings, beanbags and balls; photocopiable page 156.

In the classroom, organise the children into their colour-coded groups and discuss with them what changes they think might occur in their breathing as a result of vigorous activity. Ask: *Will your breathing stay the same? How will you find out?*

What to do

(5 mins) Warm-up

In a space, ask the children to put one hand on their chest and one hand on their tummy and feel their breathing. Then ask them to jog on the spot and gradually increase the speed of the action. Encourage using the arms and lifting the knees. Keep varying the pace of the action.

Then ask them to do this as they move about the playground looking for spaces. Remind them to look where they are going as they move in and out of each other.

Introduce the game 'Two, one, other' (see photocopiable page 156). In this game, the children jog in and out using all the space and when you say *Two*, they touch the ground with two hands and then keep jogging. When you say *One*, they touch the ground with one hand and then keep jogging. When you say *Other*, they touch the ground with the other hand and then keep jogging. Repeat several times, varying the instructions.

Now ask everyone to stop in a space and then to put their hands on their tummy and chest to feel their breathing. What do they notice?

(10 mins) Development

Ask the children to walk to their colour-coded basket, collect a rubber ring and stand with it in a space.

Ask them to pass the ring from hand to hand in front of them. Point out the grasping and releasing actions and emphasise closing their hands around the ring. Encourage the children to think of another place they can pass the ring from hand to hand (above their heads, between their legs, in front of their knees, behind their backs and so on). Observe the different responses from the children and then select some for them all to try.

Encourage them to try passing the ring around different parts of their bodies (such as knees, ankles, head and waist – see Diagram 1) and to try these in the other direction.

Diagram 1

Learning objectives
● Become familiar with handling rubber rings – carrying, spinning, passing from hand to hand.
● Explore the changes that occur in breathing rate as a result of vigorous activity.
● Practise individually with selected pieces of equipment.

Lesson organisation
Teacher-led classroom discussion; individual exercises; teacher-led classroom review.

Vocabulary
breathing rate
vigorous activity
steer
reverse
brake
pouncing
above
between
behind
in front of
spinning

Encourage more able children to gradually increase the speed at which they do this to give them a challenge.

Make a game of this by saying *Change* and asking the children to respond to this by changing the place where they are passing the ring. Try to speed this up gradually.

Ask the children to put the ring on the floor in a space and then to walk around it. Encourage them to go in both directions. See if they can keep close to the ring with very little steps and then to try to make a larger circle around the ring.

Introduce the car game (see photocopiable page 156). Ask the children to hold their rings like a steering wheel and to jog in and out of all the spaces. Advise them of the instructions:

● Stop – brake and stop still.
● Start – move forward.
● Change – change direction.
● Reverse – move backwards.

With their rings on the ground in a space, ask the children to jump over their rings without touching them. Ask them to have a go at this in different directions (side to side, forwards and backwards) and to practise it.

Ask the children to try to spin the ring on the floor. Encourage them to try spinning it in both directions, and help them to do this by demonstrating a twist and release action. Ask them to try this using both hands or each hand in turn and to stop the ring before it stops turning by pouncing on it. Encourage them to think of and try another action that they can do before it stops spinning (jumping over it, walking around it, clapping their hands twice and so on).

Invite them to choose something else that they want to practise with the ring. Help them to set their own challenges: How many times in a row can they successfully collect the ring? Can they beat their own records?

Games

Explain to the children that now they are going to choose one piece of equipment to play and practise with. Ask them to return their rubber rings to their baskets and to choose one piece of equipment from beanbags, rings, large or small balls. Tell them to take it into a space and start to practise using it.

Encourage and challenge the children individually as they practise (for example to see how many catches they can make before they drop the beanbag or if they can dribble the ball up to a line and back again without it rolling away). Ask them to count and try to beat their record or to make their action a little more difficult (a bit higher, further away, with the other hand and so on).

To finish, tell everyone to return the equipment to the correct baskets and collect a ring each.

Cool-down

In a space, ask each child to place a ring on their head and to walk around, trying not to let the ring fall off. Ask them all to try to change direction and to keep moving using all the spaces. Ask them to try to bend down to touch the floor as they do this. Encourage them to bend their knees and let the children practise this several times.

Tell them to pass the ring around their bodies and then place it on the floor in front of them. Ask two of the groups to walk around and collect the rings for their baskets, then ask the other two groups to do the same.

Classroom review

Ask the children what they noticed about their breathing when they stopped after doing lots of jogging and playing the game 'Two, one, other'. Discuss breathing rates. Was their rate what they had expected it to be?

Differentiation

More able children can be challenged to gradually increase the speed at which they pass the rings, and should be encouraged to provide original responses and ideas.

Encourage, help and challenge children individually as much as you can.

Assessing learning outcomes

Are the children able to sustain vigorous activity? Can they manipulate and handle the rings well?

30 mins Can we try more ways of using the rings?

What you need and preparation

You will need: colour-coded baskets of equipment, including rings, beanbags and balls; photocopiable page 156.

In the classroom, remind the children of their groups. Discuss how they used the rings last week, and ask them to think what they might like to try in this lesson.

What to do

6 mins Warm-up

Ask the children to jog on the spot and then jog around the playground looking for spaces. Remind them of, and play the game, 'Two, one, other' (see photocopiable page 156). Encourage them to notice their breathing rate when they have played for several minutes.

Ask them in groups to collect a ring each from the baskets, ready to play the car game (see photocopiable page 156). Ask them to jog around the playground using their ring like a steering wheel to guide them into all the spaces. Remind them of the instructions *Stop, Start, Change* and *Reverse*. Ask them which directions they could move in and what they need to remember, particularly when they are moving backwards. Check that they are looking behind them when they move backwards.

Explain the game 'Stop and go' (see photocopiable page 156). Ask the children to hold their ring and to move around the playground into spaces, listening for your instructions.

Make sure the children look where they are going and use all the spaces.

10 mins Development

Ask the children to put their rings on the ground in space and to notice where their ring is in relation to other things or people. *What is it near or opposite?* See if they can remember where their ring is when they jog away from it and to return to it when you say *Home*. Start when they are only a short distance away and then encourage them to jog in and out of the rings going all around the hall or playground.

Ask the children to think of different ways in which they can pick up their rings. Encourage them to be inventive and to use various parts of their bodies to do this. Observe their responses and choose a few of their ideas for everyone to practise (for example they could use their elbows, one foot, both feet, one finger).

Ask them all to jump over their rings without touching them, then to do this in different directions (side to side, forwards and backwards) and to practise this.

Next, ask the children to drop their ring flat on the floor and to watch it and then pick it up. Can they bounce their ring? What happens when they drop it on its edge? Ask them to drop it in a different way (such as on its edge or from a different height) and to watch it and collect it quickly.

Let the children think of and practise other ways in which they can use their rings. Encourage, help and challenge them individually.

Learning objectives
● Make good use of space.
● Practise putting down, picking up and carrying rings in different ways.
● Practise different ways of passing rings individually and in pairs, and make up a game with a partner.

Lesson organisation
Teacher-led classroom discussion; individual warm-up; individual and paired work with rings; games in pairs; whole-class cool-down; teacher-led classroom review.

Vocabulary
breathing rate
reverse
brake

In pairs, ask the children to stand close to their partner and to practise passing the ring backwards and forwards to each other (not throwing to begin with). Encourage different positions in which this can be done (side by side, kneeling, back to back, with legs apart, over their heads and so on – see Diagram 2). Encourage them to begin to stand a bit further apart and speed up the passing.

Diagram 2

Games

10 mins Challenge the pairs to count how many passes they can make without dropping the ring and to try this passing in different ways.

Ask them to make up a game of passing, making sure that they have fair turns.

Ask the children to return their rings to the baskets and to choose one piece of equipment each from beanbags, rings, large or small balls. Ask them to take that object into a space and practise using it. Encourage and challenge the children individually as they practise. For example, they could count and try to beat their record, or make their action more difficult (a bit higher, from a little further away, with the other hand and so on).

Cool-down

4 mins Back in their pairs, ask one member from each pair to collect two rings from the basket and give one to their partner so they have one each. Ask them to place a ring on their heads, like they did in the last lesson, and to walk around in a space trying not to let the ring fall off. Encourage them to try changing direction and keep moving, using all the spaces. Ask them to try to bend down to touch the floor as they do this. Encourage them to bend their knees and practise this several times.

Explain the game 'Help each other' (see photocopiable page 156). With their rings on their heads they are to walk around, using all the spaces, again, trying not to let the rings fall off. This time, if it falls off their head they stand still and put their hands up until someone comes to help them. They are not allowed to put it back on themselves, but anyone else can bend down, pick it up and put it on their head for them. Ask everyone to see how many other children they can help without their own ring falling off. If someone helping loses their ring then they wait for help too. Stop frequently to start again.

After a while, ask all the children to stretch and hold their ring up as high as they can and then to move it gently from side to side in the air.

Tell them to pass the ring around their bodies and then place it on the floor in front of them.

Ask two groups to collect and put their equipment away in the baskets, then ask the other two to do the same.

Classroom review

Were the children able to beat their own records (number of catches and passes)? What help did they need? Discuss the different ways they found to pass the ring to each other.

Did they like the game 'Help each other'? Were they able to help each other put their rings back on their heads? How did they manage to keep their rings on their heads?

Differentiation

Expect original responses from the more able and encourage and help the less able. Encourage, help and challenge children individually as they practise.

Assessing learning outcomes

Are the children making good use of space? Are they showing an awareness of others? Are they handling the rings with more confidence and control?

(30 mins) What ways of passing the ring can we try?

What you need and preparation

You will need: colour-coded baskets containing rings, beanbags and balls; photocopiable page 156.

Discuss with the children different ways in which they can pass a ring to each other. Focus specifically on rolling and throwing and catching. Organise them into their groups.

What to do

(5 mins) Warm-up

Ask the children to jog on the spot and then in and out of the space, stopping when you give the instruction. Play the game 'Two, one, other' (see photocopiable page 156) for a few minutes until they are thoroughly warm and breathing hard. Ask them to notice their breathing rate and then collect a ring from the basket, taking lots of deep breaths as they go.

Play 'Stop and go' (see photocopiable page 156), asking the children to hold their rings as they jog around. Remind them that they should keep moving all the time, jogging on the spot when their ring is on the floor. Encourage them to alternate which hand they use and sometimes to use both hands to do this.

Introduce another aspect of the game by explaining to the children that this time, instead of picking up their own ring, you want them to pick up someone else's and then keep jogging. Continue to play 'Stop and go' in this way, encouraging the children to look for the free rings and use all the space.

(10 mins) Development

Ask the children to put their rings flat on the floor and to try stepping over them in different directions. Encourage sideways jumping, then encourage lots of different ways of jumping over their rings without touching them. Encourage them all to try using one foot or two (hopping; leaping or jumping from two feet to two feet).

Ask the children to take their ring into a space and to practise spinning it on the floor. Encourage them to try spinning it in both directions using both hands or each hand in turn. Invite them to practise an action that they can do before it stops spinning (perhaps jumping over it, walking around it, clapping their hands twice and so on).

Ask everyone to roll their ring and walk alongside it, picking it up before it bumps into anyone or anything else. Ask the children to see if they can keep the ring rolling by using lots of little taps to maintain momentum.

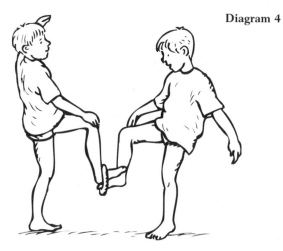

Now ask each of the children to stand in a space, throw their ring into the air (at about head height) and catch it, grasping it with both hands. Ask them to try it again with just one hand.

Organise the children into pairs. Ask one of each pair to put their ring away in the basket and then to stand or sit with their partner. Tell everyone to practise rolling the remaining ring backwards and forwards together, keeping it on the ground.

12 mins Games

Ask the children, in their pairs, to make up a game of rolling the ring to each other, thinking about different positions in which they could do this (standing, kneeling, back to back with legs apart and so on). Tell them to count how many times they can roll the ring to each other without it going astray. Encourage them to keep trying to beat their record.

Diagram 3

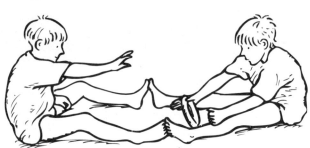

Next, ask the children to stand close to their partners and to practise passing the ring backwards and forwards to each other. Invite them to think of several different ways. Encourage different positions in which this can be done (such as side by side, kneeling, back to back, with legs apart or over their heads – see Diagram 3).

Ask them to create a passing game with their partner in which the ring must not touch the floor. Remind them to think about different positions in which they could do this (see Diagram 4, for example).

Ask them to count how many times they can pass it to each other without dropping the ring. Again, encourage them to keep trying to beat their record.

Now ask all the children to return their rings to the baskets and to choose one piece of equipment each to practise with. Tell everyone to take their equipment into a space and to start to practise using it.

Encourage and challenge the children individually as they practise. They could, for example, count and try to beat their record or make their action more difficult (for example throwing it higher, from a little further away, with the other hand).

Diagram 4

3 mins Cool-down

Ask the children with beanbag and rings to keep them, but everyone who was working with a ball to return it to the basket, choosing a ring or beanbag instead. Once everyone is in a space, with a beanbag or ring, remind the class of the game 'Help each other' (see photocopiable page 156) and tell them to start moving around, keeping their objects on their heads for as long as possible. Remind them that if their beanbag or ring does fall off, they are not allowed to put it back themselves, but must put their hands up and quietly wait for help. Advise them to look for people who are waiting for assistance as they walk around, and to see how many people they can help.

After a short while, ask the children to spread out again and stand still in their space. Ask them to stretch up and hold their ring or beanbag up as high as they can and then to move it gently from side to side in the air.

Encourage them to pass the ring or beanbag around their bodies and then place it on the floor in front of them. Finish by asking all those with a beanbag to walk and put these in the baskets, then ask those with a ring to do the same.

Classroom review
Discuss with the children how many different ways they found to roll or pass the ring to their partners. What happened when they tried to roll their ring in a straight line?

Differentiation
Encourage those who can catch the ring with one hand to try it with their other hand.

Assessing learning outcomes
Are the children making good use of space? Are they showing an awareness of others? How well are they able to manage rolling and passing the ring?

(30 mins) Can we use hoops?

What you need and preparation
You will need colour-coded baskets containing rings, beanbags, balls and hoops for each child.

What to do
(6 mins) Warm-up
Ask the children to jog around the playground in different directions, using all the spaces.

Ask them all to collect a hoop and put it quietly on the floor in a space. Then ask them to stand in it and bring it up and over their head, then practise lowering it down as gently as possible again without making a sound. Practise this movement together several times.

Ask the children to jog carefully around the hoops without touching them and when they hear you say *Stop*, to go and stand in a hoop the same colour as theirs. Do this several times and then ask them to go to any hoop. Gradually take away a few hoops at a time but instead of being 'out', the children have to *share* fewer and fewer hoops. Encourage them to help each other to do this. When there are only about six hoops left, play the game again, this time replacing the hoops until everyone has one each again.

(10 mins) Development
Standing in their hoops, ask the children to lift their hoops over their heads and to put them down on the ground again as quickly as possible. Repeat several times.

From the same starting position, ask them to jump in and out of their hoops using both feet. Encourage them to go all around the edge of the hoop, jumping in and out. Encourage them to try that in different ways (forwards and backwards or side to side). Pick out some good examples for everyone to try. Then ask everyone to make a pattern of jumps. Practise and repeat the pattern together.

Ask the children to show you what else they can do with their hoops. Allow free practice for a few minutes and then select one or two children trying to hula-hoop to demonstrate it.

Encourage them all to hula-hoop by spinning the hoops around their waists.

(12 mins) Games
Ask the children to return their hoops to the baskets and to choose one piece of equipment from beanbags, rings, balls or hoops. Ask them to take their object into a space and practise with it.

Learning objectives
● Practise jumping patterns in and out of a hoop.
● Try different ways of turning a hoop around the body.
● Try to intercept a partner as they run from one side of the playground to another.

Lesson organisation
Individual practice and challenges; games in pairs; individual cool-down; teacher-led classroom review.

Vocabulary
hula-hoop
spinning

Encourage and challenge the children individually as they practise. For example, can they count and try to beat their record or make their action a little more difficult than last time?

Ask everyone to return their equipment tidily to the baskets and then to stand with a partner, numbering themselves 1 and 2.

In pairs, play 'Farmer, may we cross your river?' Explain that number 1 stands on a line at one side of the playground (to represent one side of the river). At the other side of the playing area use or draw a parallel line (the other side of the river) at least five metres from any wall, fence or boundary. Number 2 stands between the two lines and moves to prevent number 1 from crossing to the other side. The purpose for number 1 is to reach the other side without being touched. Emphasise that the catcher does not just chase but tries to intercept (moving from side to side). Let the pairs practise several times, taking it in turns to be the farmer (catcher).

(2 mins) Cool-down
Ask all the children to jog slowly, then walk around the space, using different directions.

Classroom review
Ask the children to describe some of the ways they used their hoop.

Assessing learning outcomes
Were the children able to repeat jumping patterns in their hoops? How well did they manage the hula-hoop?

(30 mins) Can we develop our actions with the hoop?

What you need and preparation
You will need: colour-coded baskets of rings, beanbags, balls and hoops; photocopiable page 157.

What to do
(5 mins) Warm-up
Ask the children to jog on the spot, then around the space, gradually building up, then alternating the speed (fast–slow–fast).

Ask them to collect a hoop each and to put it quietly on the floor in a space. Ask them to jog carefully around the hoops without touching them and when they hear you say *Stop*, to go and stand in a hoop. Try this with numbers. When you say *Three*, three children stand in a hoop. When you say *Four*, that number of children stand in the hoop. Practise this several times and then ask the children to listen carefully to the new instructions.

Play 'Parts of the body in the hoop'. Give an example – when you say *Seven elbows*, you want seven elbows in a hoop and that this could be seven children with one elbow each in the hoop or any combination of four, five or six. Repeat the game with other suggestions, such as three bottoms, 35 fingers, five hands, four feet and so on, to suit the group of children.

(12 mins) Development
Ask the children to take a hoop each and hold it upright. See how quickly they can move through the hoop from one side to the other.

Ask them to roll the hoop into a space and to run and collect it. Observe the different ways they do this and then encourage them all to try holding the top with one hand and then pushing from behind with the other hand. Encourage them to look for a space before they push and to try to stop it before it bumps into anyone.

Exploring rings and hoops

Vocabulary
fingers
bottoms
heads
elbows
sending
rolling
receiving
follow-through

Ask them to try to keep the hoop rolling continuously by using lots of little taps while walking alongside it. Ask them if they can keep it straight.

In pairs, ask one partner to return their hoop to the corner. With one hoop between two, ask them to roll the hoop to their partner. Encourage partners to stand ready and to move to collect the hoop. Advise the children rolling the hoop to stand sideways and to aim for their partner's hands. See how many times they can roll the hoop without it rolling away.

Now tell everyone to leave their hoops on the floor and ask one member of each pair to go to their basket and collect a beanbag. Ask the pairs to stand three small steps away from their hoop and to throw their beanbag underarm into the hoop. Encourage a good follow-through with fingers pointing towards the hoop as the beanbag is released. Encourage stepping forward onto the left foot if they are throwing with their right hand, and with the right foot if they are left-handed. Tell them to practise this several times, taking a small step backwards after being successful, and a small step forwards if the beanbag misses the hoop.

Ask everyone to try to think of, and practise, several other ways of throwing the beanbag into the hoop.

⑩ Games

Ask the children to return their hoops to the baskets and to choose one piece of equipment from beanbags, rings, large or small balls and to practise using it. Encourage and challenge the children individually as they practise. For example, they could count and try to beat their record or make their action more difficult.

Ask everyone to return their equipment tidily to the baskets and then to stand by a partner, numbering themselves 1 and 2.

Play 'Farmer, may we cross your river?' Remind the children of how the game is played. Number 1 stands on a line at one side of the playground (one side of the river). Number 2 stands between number 1 and the other side of the playground to prevent them from crossing to the other side. The purpose for number 1 is to reach the other side without being caught. After each person has had the chance to be the farmer, ask them to think of ways in which they might get across. Encourage them to pretend to move one way and then suddenly move the other way to get past their partner.

③ Cool-down

Play 'Back to front' (see photocopiable page 157), still in pairs. Explain that, in this game, number 1 leads and number 2 follows, jogging slowly about the space. On your command, *Back to front*, the person following jogs in front of their partner and becomes the leader, slowing jogging and leading their partner in and out of the spaces and away from other pairs. Only one rule should need to be applied – no crossing between another pair. Try this for a while then tell the children to slow down and change to walking.

Ask everyone to move into their own space and stretch and relax to finish.

Classroom review
Ask the children what helped them to get past their partner in the farmer game.

Assessing learning outcomes
Were the children able to roll and collect a hoop successfully? Did they manage to think of ways to get past their partner in the farmer game?

Exploring rings
and hoops

30 **Can we skip with a hoop?**
mins

Learning objectives
● Practise the hula-hoop.
● Jump in and out of a hoop held near the ground by a partner.
● Practise skipping with a hoop.
● Roll a hoop in different ways.
● Be mindful of others when using hoops.

Lesson organisation
Individual warm-up; individual, then paired activities using hoops; individual and paired games; paired cool-down; teacher-led classroom review.

Vocabulary
turning
rolling
skipping
dodging
flick of the wrist
backspin
dodge

What you need and preparation
You will need: colour-coded baskets with hoops, beanbags, rings and balls; photocopiable page 157.

What to do

5 mins Warm-up
Ask the children to collect a hoop each and to show you their hula-hoop. After some practise, ask them to put the hoop quietly on the floor in a space. Ask them to jog carefully around the hoops, without touching them, and when they hear you say *Stop*, to go and stand in a hoop.

Play 'Parts of the body in the hoop'. Remind them how to play and give an example – when you say *Five feet*, you want five feet in a hoop (this could be five children with one foot each in the hoop). Repeat with other suggestions, such as three bottoms, 35 fingers, four hands, four feet and so on, to suit the abilities of the children.

12 mins Development
Ask the children to practise hula-hooping, turning the hoop in both directions.

Tell them to try turning the hoop around them in a different way. Watch for examples and use a few as demonstrations. Then ask everyone to turn the hoop over their heads as if it were a skipping rope (see Diagrams 5 and 6). Practise, and help the children to step over and turn the hoop, keeping the rhythm going. Challenge them to beat their record, counting the number of times they can turn and jump over the hoop without stopping.

Diagram 5

In pairs, ask them to practise rolling a hoop for their partner to catch. Then ask them to try rolling the hoop so that it comes back to them. Try a flick of the wrist upwards (backspin) to make the hoop roll away and then roll back again.

Still in pairs, with one hoop between two, ask one child to hold the hoop horizontally at ankle height out to the side of them. Their partner then jumps in and out several times. Remind them to change over frequently, say after five jumps, so that all the children have fair turns. Try different ways of doing this (one foot or two feet take off, different directions) and then gradually raise the height of the hoop a little.

10 mins Games
Ask the children to return their hoops to their baskets and to choose one piece of equipment from beanbags, rings, large or small balls. Ask them to take that into a space and start to practise using it. Encourage and challenge the children individually as they practise. For example, they could count and try to beat their record of consecutive successful actions or make their action more difficult (higher, further away, using the other hand and so on).

Now ask everyone to return their equipment tidily to the baskets and stand with a partner behind a specified line.

In twos, play 'Farmer, may we cross your river?' Remind the children how to play (see page 102). Encourage the children to try to dodge past their partner into a space on the other side. Emphasise that the catcher does not just chase but tries to intercept.

Cool-down

3 mins Play 'Back to front' (see photocopiable page 157). Remind the children that number 1 leads and number 2 follows, jogging slowly about the space. Advise them to listen out for *Back to front*, when the child following overtakes their partner and becomes the leader, then slows and leads their partner in and out of the spaces and away from other pairs. Again, after a while, ask the children to slow down and change to walking.

Finish by asking the children all to find a space in which to stretch and relax.

Diagram 6

Classroom review

Ask the children to describe how they tried to skip with their hoops. What did they like doing with their hoops best? What have they learned to do in the last few weeks that they could not do before?

Differentiation

For those who can skip easily with a hoop, encourage them to:
● try turning it backwards
● speed up the turn
● try different ways of jumping or stepping over the hoop as they skip.
  Less able children should be encouraged to practise simple skipping with the hoop.

Assessing learning outcomes

How well can the children skip with a hoop? Are they mindful of others as they use their hoops?

Jumping, skipping and bouncing

This unit will engage children in lots of cardiovascular activity, exploration and practise. They will practise and consolidate the basic skills of running, jumping and bouncing in a variety of contexts and develop their skipping skills, starting with something most children can be successful with – jumping over a rope on the ground.

The aim is for as much activity and practise as is possible, in a variety of situations, and therefore sufficient equipment should be available for one piece each.

UNIT: Jumping, skipping and bouncing

Enquiry questions	Learning objectives	Teaching activities	Learning outcomes
What jumping patterns can we make?	● Create a pattern of jumps over a rope, forwards, sideways and backwards. ● Practise running and jumping over a rope in different ways. ● Try different ways of bouncing and catching a ball.	Warm-up: jogging on the spot with varying speeds; practising stopping and starting; playing 'Find your partner'. Development: practising with one piece of equipment; jumping over a rope; making pattern of jumps; copying partner's pattern; practising skipping with a rope; tapping and bouncing a ball along the ground. Games: making up a game of bouncing with a partner; playing the numbers game. Cool-down: walking along lines, heel to toe; stretching and relaxing.	Children: ● repeat their pattern of jumps ● copy their partners' patterns
How can we practise jumping and bouncing?	● Create a pattern of jumps in a rope circle and copy a partner's pattern. ● Practise different ways of bouncing a ball using a rope circle.	Warm-up: jogging about the space; playing 'Follow my leader'. Development: practising with one piece of equipment; jumping over a rope with two feet; making a pattern of jumps and repeating; copying partner's pattern; dribbling a ball with feet; bouncing a ball in and around ropes. Games: making up a game of bouncing with a partner; playing 'Numbers'. Cool-down: walking quickly and gradually slowing down.	● remember and record their pattern of jumps ● bounce the ball and beat their own records
Can we jump far and controll a bouncing ball?	● Practise jumping patterns, individually and in pairs. ● Practise a standing jump for distance (inside, outside and over a rope circle). ● Try different ways of bouncing a ball.	Warm-up: jumping up and down in different ways; making pattern of jumps; playing 'Follow my leader'. Development: practising with one piece of equipment; jumping over a rope circle with two feet; bouncing a ball in a rope circle; making a pattern of bounces. Games: copying partner's pattern of bounces; practising jumping and skipping individually. Cool-down: jogging with a partner, gradually slowing; stretching and relaxing.	● use their arms to help them jump for distance ● bounce the ball in different ways
Can we play 'Follow my leader' with balls and ropes?	● Copy a partner's pattern of jumps. ● Practise a standing jump, gradually increasing the distance jumped. ● Practise skipping over a moving rope. ● Catch a bouncing ball in different positions. ● Estimate strides and hops across a set distance.	Warm-up: playing 'Follow my leader'. Development: practising with one piece of equipment; tiptoeing, jumping and hopping around rope shape; playing 'widening river' and 'hopscotch'; practising ways of bouncing around rope shape. Games: following a partner who is bouncing the ball; making up a game with a partner using a ball and a rope circle; practising jumping and skipping. Cool-down: jogging then slow-motion jogging.	● describe their actions to their partners ● co-operate to make up a game

UNIT: Jumping, skipping and bouncing

Enquiry questions	Learning objectives	Teaching activities	Learning outcomes
Can we beat our skipping and bouncing records?	● Practise stopping, starting and changing direction suddenly. ● Practise skipping and jumping, making individual challenges. ● Create a pattern of bounces. ● Co-operate in different ways with a partner.	Warm-up: walking then jogging around the space; stopping and starting; playing 'Body parts'. Development: practising with one piece of equipment; jumping over moving rope; jumping over two ropes; rolling a ball between parallel lines for a partner to field; gathering and stopping the ball. Games: making up a game with a partner using a rope and a ball; bouncing and skipping; bouncing the ball in turns. Cool-down: leading a partner whose eyes are closed around the space.	● co-operate with each other ● take fair turns
What different ways of skipping can we try?	● Practise skipping. ● Practise using a ball and rope together.	Warm-up: jogging then running with increased speed; practising stopping; playing 'Body parts'. Development: practising with one piece of equipment; swaying and skipping in threes; practising jumping, skipping and bouncing. Games: practising skipping with skipping rhymes. Cool-down: taking it in turns to lead and be led (follower has eyes closed).	● progress with their skipping ● develop the rhythm of the action.

Cross-curricular links
Maths: estimating and making rough measurements of distances.

Resources
Ropes; colour-coded baskets with hoops, rings, beanbags, balls of different sizes; a whistle; a stopwatch; photocopiable pages 157 and 158; paper; writing materials.

(30 mins) What jumping patterns can we make?

What you need and preparation

You will need: four colour-coded baskets of equipment containing enough ropes, balls beanbags and hoops for one each; photocopiable page 157.

Discuss with the children in the classroom the arrangements for listening and using the space while outside.

Organise the children into four colour-coded groups.

What to do

(5 mins) Warm-up

Ask the children to jog on the spot and then vary the speed of the action – faster, slower, faster and so on. Ask them to jog in and out of each other around the playground, looking for all the spaces. Practise stopping and starting.

Explain to the children how to play 'Find your partner' (see photocopiable page 157). Ask them to find a partner and to shake hands. Then ask the pairs to move away from each other. Tell them all to jog in and out of everyone else around the playground, using the middle and the edges of the space, keeping away from their partner. On your *Stop* signal, tell them to find their partner and crouch down together in a space. Repeat, then tell the children to change partners and try again.

(12 mins) Development

Ask the children to go to their baskets and choose one piece of equipment to practise with. Challenge them individually as they practise.

Then tell them to return their equipment and collect a skipping rope each. Ask the children to lay their rope down on the floor in a straight line in a space. Ask them to jump over their rope in different ways. Look for good examples of the use of different directions and choose children to demonstrate jumping backwards and forwards over the rope and then jumping from side to side over the rope. Ask everyone to try with two feet and then with one foot after another. See if the children can make a pattern of jumps (for example side to side, side to side, backwards and forwards).

In pairs, ask the children to show their patterns to their partners and see if their partners can copy it. Ask the pairs to swap roles. Can they make up a pattern together? Can they practise it at the same time?

With ropes lying in straight lines all over the playground, ask the children to run around the whole space, jumping over ropes when they come to them. Encourage them and use demonstrations to illustrate a leaping action, helping the children to land softly, one foot after the other.

Ask all the children to practise turning an imaginary rope as if they were skipping. Emphasise holding their arms up and out and turning the rope in big circles with a regular rhythm (see Diagram 7).

Diagram 7

Now tell everyone to pick up their rope and to hold each end of the rope. Take them through this procedure: *Starting with the middle of the rope behind the heels, turn it over your head so that it lands on the floor in front of you. Step over it and turn it again so that you are walking forwards with a rope.* Encourage the children to walk over the rope as soon as it touches the ground and to keep the rope turning. For those who can skip, encourage them to increase the speed of their skip and skip forward.

Then ask the children to put down their ropes and collect a medium-sized ball. Tell them to start by tapping the ball along the ground around the rope, stopping and starting, and changing direction.

Ask the children to try bouncing their ball in different ways around their rope. Look for good examples of different ways to use for demonstration. Ask the others to try some of the ways they have seen (using two hands, pat-bouncing, using alternate hands and so on).

(10 mins) Games

Ask the children to make up a game in pairs using one ball between two.

Ask everyone to put the balls and the ropes away. Play the numbers game – in which you call a number and the children have to get into groups of that number.

(3 mins) Cool-down

Ask the children to find a line in the playground and to walk along it, keeping their feet on the line. Encourage them to try walking putting heel to toe forwards then backwards, then try sideways with just their toes on the line.

Ask them to move into a space to stretch and relax before returning the baskets to the store.

Classroom review

Ask the children if they thought of three ways to bounce their ball. Can they tell a partner about their pattern of jumps?

Assessing learning outcomes

Could the children repeat their pattern of jumps? Could they copy their partner's pattern?

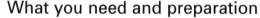

(30 mins) How can we practise jumping and bouncing?

Learning objectives
● Create a pattern of jumps in a rope circle and copy a partner's pattern.
● Practise different ways of bouncing a ball using a rope circle.

Lesson organisation
Individual and paired warm-up and practice; paired games; individual cool-down; teacher-led classroom review.

What you need and preparation

You will need four colour-coded baskets of equipment, including sufficient ropes and small/medium balls for one each; paper and writing materials (for the classroom review).

Organise the children into four colour-coded groups.

What to do

(5 mins) Warm-up

Ask the children to jog about the space, moving lightly on their feet. Encourage them to use lots of curving pathways in and out of everyone else, keeping in a big space.

Play 'Follow my leader' in pairs. Explain that the leader jogs around the space in an interesting pathway while their partner follows their actions. Remind them to keep changing over to ensure fair turns. Encourage them to change the speed, going a little faster or a little slower.

(15 mins) Development

Ask the children to go to the baskets and to choose and practise with one piece of equipment. Challenge them individually to improve their actions.

Now ask the children to collect one skipping rope each from the baskets and to make a circle with their rope on the floor in a space. Ask them to try different ways of jumping over their rope. Look for good examples and use demonstrations to illustrate jumping in the middle of the shape, around the outside, in and out, sideways and backwards. Tell them to make up a pattern of jumps (for example apart, together, apart, together, together; hop, hop, jump, jump, jump; side to middle, side to middle). Ask them if they can repeat the pattern twice, four times, then ten times.

In pairs, ask the children to show their patterns to their partners and see if their partners can copy them. Ask them to change over, the first child trying their partner's pattern. Can they repeat it? What would be the third movement – a hop or a jump? Can they find a way to try to remember or record the pattern?

Now ask everyone to get a medium-sized ball and dribble it with their feet around the outside of the shape. Encourage the children to follow the contours of the shape, keeping the ball as close to the rope as they can. Then ask them to try it a little more quickly, without letting the ball run away. Tell them to dribble the ball in and out around the space without letting it touch any of the ropes.

Next, ask the children to try the same dribbling action, but using their hands instead of their feet. Remind them to be aware of where they are going, but to otherwise keep their eyes on the ball. Invite them to practise this a few times.

Ask the children to practise bouncing the ball in the rope circle. Encourage them by asking: *Can you beat your record?*

8 mins **Games**
Ask the children to make up a game with their partner using one ball between two and one rope. Play the numbers game (see Games on page 110).

2 mins **Cool-down**
Ask the children to walk quickly around the space and then encourage them to gradually slow down.

Classroom review
Ask the children to think about their pattern of jumps. Can they try out a way of recording their pattern on a piece of paper? Can they show and explain it to a partner?

Assessing learning outcomes
Are the children able to remember and record their pattern of jumps? How successful are they in bouncing the ball and beating their record?

20 mins Can we jump far and control a bouncing ball?

What you need and preparation
You will need: four colour-coded baskets of equipment, including enough ropes and balls for one of each for each child; photocopiable page 157.

Organise the children into four colour-coded groups.

What to do
6 mins **Warm-up**
Ask the children to jump up and down on the spot and then to try some different ways of jumping (for example astride and together, hopping, leaping and so on). Ask them to practise these and to make a simple pattern of jumps.

Learning objectives
● Practise jumping patterns, individually and in pairs
● Practise a standing jump for distance (inside, outside and over a rope circle).
● Try different ways of bouncing a ball.

**Jumping, skipping
and bouncing**

**Lesson
organisation**
Individual and
paired warm-up;
individual and
paired practice;
paired games;
paired cool-down;
teacher-led
classroom review.

Vocabulary
astride
together
follow my leader

Organise the children into pairs to play 'Follow my leader' (see photocopiable page 157), using jumps and hops. Explain that you want the leader to explain and describe to their partner their first move (for example jumping with both feet together, hopping for a number of hops then changing legs) then demonstrate that action. The second child then joins in, following all their partner's actions. Tell them to change over, ensuring fair turns.

5 mins Development

Ask the children to go to the baskets and to choose and practise with one piece of equipment.

Then ask them to collect a skipping rope and to make a circle with it on the floor. Ask them to stand on one side of the rope with their toes close to it. With a two-footed jump, ask them to crouch and jump as far as they can. Ask them to turn around on the spot and then see if they can jump back over the rope. Try several times, encouraging them to swing their arms to help them jump (see diagram 8).

Diagram 8

With one ball and one rope each, ask the children to practise bouncing the ball in different ways in the middle of the rope circle. Encourage different ways of bouncing and challenge them to beat their own record.

Now ask them to try bouncing the ball around the *inside* edge of the circle without it touching the rope, then the *outside* edge, keeping it as close to the rope as possible without touching it.

Finally, ask them to try to make a pattern of bounces using their rope circle (for example inside, outside, outside).

6 mins Games

Ask the children to get into pairs, and number themselves 1 and 2. Ask number 1 to show their partner their pattern of bounces and number 2 to try to copy the pattern. Make sure that they then swap over to ensure fair turns.

Ask everyone to put their balls away and then to practise jumping and skipping on their own. Encourage and challenge them individually.

3 mins Cool-down

Ask the children to jog with a partner, taking it in turns to lead and to follow, gradually slowing down to stretch and relax.

Classroom review

Ask the children: *How did you try to bounce the ball? Did you beat your own record of bouncing the ball?*

Assessing learning outcomes

Did the children use their arms to help them jump for distance? Could they bounce the ball in different ways?

(30 mins) Can we play 'Follow my leader' with balls and ropes?

What you need and preparation
You will need: four colour-coded baskets of equipment, including enough ropes and small/medium balls for one each; photocopiable page 157.

Organise the children into four colour-coded groups.

What to do
(5 mins) Warm-up
Ask the children to start by hopping individually around the space. Remind them to be aware of the others around them and to look for open spaces.

Then organise them into pairs and remind them how to play 'Follow my leader' (see photocopiable page 157). Encourage the leaders to use different movements from last time, and make sure they change over and take fair turns.

(12 mins) Development
Ask the children to go to the baskets and choose one piece of equipment to practise with. Challenge them individually to improve on what they have done before.

With ropes in a curving shape, ask the children to tiptoe alongside them as closely as they can without touching the rope. Ask: *How many jumps does it take for you to get from one end to the other?* Ask them to estimate:

- how many hops
- how many strides
- how many pigeon steps.

With the ropes in 'V' shapes, play 'Widening river'. Tell the children to start by jumping over the pointed end of the 'V', and then jump over the rope as it gradually gets wider. Ask: *Can you jump over its widest part?* Ask them to measure the widest part they jumped over using either feet or hand spans.

Ask the children to collect a ball from their basket, putting their ropes back, and practise different ways of bouncing around their rope shape (for example bouncing high and low; using two hands and then one; cupped hands or tap bouncing).

Ask them all to try tap bouncing the ball on the floor. Encourage the children to create their own challenges (for example to keep the ball bouncing). Ask them:

- How many taps can you manage?
- Can you keep the ball bouncing while you are moving?
- Can you throw it against a wall, let it bounce and then catch it?

(10 mins) Games
Ask the children to form pairs and number themselves 1 and 2 to play 'Follow my leader' bouncing a ball. Number 1s are to be the leaders, number 2s the followers. Can the number 2s follow their partners while bouncing a ball? Can they vary the ways they do this? Remind them to change over to ensure fair turns at leading and following.

Ask one of the children from each pair to return their ball and to collect a rope from the baskets. Encourage them to make up their own game with their partners, using one ball and one rope between two. For example, they could bounce the ball in the rope circle to their partner who catches and returns it. Advise them to make sure they take it in turns and have equal goes.

To finish, let the children practise jumping and skipping on their own. Encourage and challenge them individually as they practise.

Learning objectives
- Copy a partner's pattern of jumps.
- Practise a standing jump, gradually increasing the distance jumped.
- Practise skipping over a moving rope.
- Catch a bouncing ball in different positions.
- Estimate strides and hops across a set distance.

Lesson organisation
Individual and paired warm-up; individual practice; paired games; individual cool-down; teacher-led classroom review.

Vocabulary
follow my leader
hopping
skipping
jumping
fair turns
curving shapes
estimate

3 mins Cool-down

Ask the children to jog around the space, gradually getting slower and finishing with a slow-motion jog.

Classroom review

Ask the children to report how well they estimated their jumps or hops. Did they need to do more or fewer to cross the space than they had expected?

Assessing learning outcomes

How well did the children describe their actions to their partners? Did they co-operate to make up a game?

30 mins Can we beat our skipping and bouncing records?

What you need and preparation

You will need four colour-coded baskets of equipment, including enough ropes and small/medium balls for one each; a whistle; photocopiable page 158.

Organise the children into four colour-coded groups.

What to do

5 mins Warm-up

Ask the children to walk about the space, then gradually increase their speed to jogging then running. Introduce the stop signal either by using a whistle or by calling out. Practise using the signal, ensuring that the children stop still like a statue on that command. Help them to do this by encouraging a braking action with one foot in front of the other. Introduce the body parts game (see photocopiable page 158) by demonstrating the following example. Tell the children to move around the space as before. After the stop signal, say a part of the body, for example *hands*. The children must find a partner and touch hands. Repeat using other parts of the body (knees, bottoms, elbows, toes, heels, head and so on).

12 mins Development

Ask the children to go to their baskets and then practise with one chosen piece of equipment. Challenge them individually to refine their performances.

In pairs, ask the children to get one rope between two. One player is to hold the rope and make it move like a snake along the ground. Their partner tries to jump over it while it is wiggling. Make sure they change over and, if they find themselves moving around the space, to be careful about where they are going.

Still in pairs, ask the children to get one rope each, and to lay them down parallel to each other about 20cm apart in a big space. Encourage them to take it in turns to jump over both ropes ('jumping over the river'). As they practise, encourage them to move the ropes about 2cm further apart every time they are successful or closer together if they cannot jump over them.

When the two ropes are about a metre apart, ask the pairs to collect one ball between them. Each pair should now try to roll the ball between the parallel lines without the ball touching the rope. Narrow the space between the ropes to encourage accuracy, with the partner fielding the ball when it gets to the other end. Ask the children to practise gathering and stopping the ball in different ways as their partner rolls it between the ropes. Gradually encourage speeding up the rolling action. Ensure that all the children have fair turns. Repeat, this time taking it in turns to *bounce* the ball between the parallel rope lines.

10 **Games**
mins Ask the children to make up a game with the rope and the ball, for example dribble around the side of the lines and then tap it to your partner between the lines; jump, alternating astride and together down the rope, and be ready to receive the ball from the partner who has just dribbled it around the outside. Ask them: *How many times can you run between the lines while your partner is skipping or bouncing?*

3 **Cool-down**
mins In pairs, ask one of the children to hold quite firmly on to one of their partner's arms. Ask the other one to close their eyes and to trust their partner. One child leads the other, walking around the space without touching anyone else. Explain that they are only allowed to say *Stop* and *Go* to their partner. If this is working well, ask them to speed up their walking a little and to keep changing direction. Change over so each child has the experiences of leading and being led.

Classroom review
Ask the children:
● What did it feel like when you had your eyes closed?
● Did you trust your partner?
● What would help you to feel more secure?

Assessing learning outcomes
How well did the children co-operate with each other? Did they remember to take fair turns?

30 What different ways of skipping can we try?
mins

What you need and preparation
You will need four colour-coded baskets of equipment, including enough ropes and small/medium balls for one each; a whistle; a stopwatch; photocopiable page 158.
　　Organise the children into four colour-coded groups.

What to do
5 **Warm-up**
mins Start with everyone walking about the space, then gradually increase the speed to jogging, then running. Introduce the stop signal either on your whistle or by calling out. Practise this, encouraging the children to stop still like a statue on that command. Help them to do this by encouraging a braking action with one foot in front of the other.

　　Play 'Body parts' (see photocopiable page 158). After the stop signal, say a different part of the body from last time, such as *knees*. Remind the children to find a partner and touch knees. Repeat, using other parts of the body.

12 **Development**
mins Ask the children to choose and practise with one piece of equipment each from their baskets. Challenge them individually. With a ball each, let everyone practise bouncing in different ways. Ask them to try to beat their own record.

　　In threes, ask the children to return the balls to the baskets, and get one rope between three. Two children hold an end of the rope each and sway it very gently between them. The third child tries to jump over the rope several times, trying to get to five continuous jumps. Tell them to change roles on a regular basis.

Learning objectives
● Practise skipping.
● Practise using a ball and rope together.

Lesson organisation
Individual and paired warm-up; practise individually and in threes; individual and paired games; paired cool-down; teacher-led classroom review.

Vocabulary
jumping
skipping
tapping

Jumping, skipping and bouncing

Still in threes, ask two children to turn the rope while the other one skips in the middle. Ask the children to practise their jumping and skipping. Encourage and challenge them individually.

10 mins **Games**
Encourage the children to practise skipping. Challenge the more able children while they are skipping to:

● increase the number of turns they can do
● skip using different actions while turning the rope (walk, run, hop jump)
● make a step pattern (heel tap, toe tap)
● see how many skips they can do in one minute.

Organise the children into pairs and ask them which skipping rhymes they know. Can they teach one to a partner?

3 mins **Cool-down**
Remind the children of the 'trust walk' from the previous lesson (see page 115), and ask them to try it again, with a different pathway.

Once again, ensure that they change over so each child has the experiences of leading and being led.

Classroom review

Ask the children how they are getting on with their skipping. Were they able to try some different ways to skip? Acknowledge their efforts over the past few weeks.

Assessing learning outcomes

How are the children progressing with their skipping? Are they developing the rhythm of the action?

Developing bat and ball skills

This unit focuses on introducing and developing bat and ball skills which will provide a basic foundation for both striking and fielding and net/wall games. Practise of these generic skills will help build children's confidence and competence in manipulating and controlling a ball with a bat, and prepare them for short tennis, mini-rounders, Kwik Cricket and so on, and even for games like Uni-hoc.

While exploring and practising with a bat and ball, children will be judging speed and direction and learning to manipulate and control themselves and the bat as they move around the playground or hall. Starting with the ball on the ground will enable them to be successful and to develop their skills, particularly stopping (receiving), dribbling (travelling with), rolling and striking (sending) and aiming, without the frustration of balls flying everywhere.

Putting children in groups or a team situation too soon can lead to frustration and inactivity, therefore the emphasis is on individual and paired activities where children can work at their own level. They will have opportunities to respond to challenges and compete against their own best performances, which is an important step in the acquisition and extension of their skills. They will also have the chance to develop their ability to share equipment and the space, take turns, make decisions, co-operate and create challenges with their partner – essential qualities for working with others in a team. The children will also help to devise games in which they use and consolidate their skills and develop their understanding for the need for simple rules as a basic foundation for all games.

Plastic or poly bats are light, with a short handle (shaft) and are therefore manageable for children of this age group. Padder tennis-type bats or table tennis bats could also be suitable for many of the activities.

UNIT: Developing bat and ball skills

Enquiry questions	Learning objectives	Teaching activities	Learning outcomes
In what ways can we roll, tap and stop a ball?	● Practise bouncing the ball and rolling and tapping it along the ground in different directions, both for accuracy and distance. ● Practise different ways of stopping the ball with the hands. ● Combine actions of stopping a rolling ball and returning it accurately to a partner. ● Make up a game of rolling, stopping and aiming.	Warm-up: running on the spot and around the space; playing 'Jack Frost'. Development: keeping the ball on the floor, using feet and hand as a bat, tapping it in different directions; playing 'Robbers'; rolling a ball to each other in pairs. Games: making up a game rolling the ball to a partner. Cool-down: passing the ball to a partner in different ways.	Children: ● stop, dribble and control a ball ● ensure fair turns in a game
How can we use a bat?	● Practise different ways of rolling and stopping a ball. ● Practise dribbling the ball in different pathways. ● Make up a game in twos, tapping, stopping and aiming the ball along the ground with a bat.	Warm-up: playing 'Jack Frost'. Development: rolling and stopping the ball; playing 'Change'; practising different ways of running and retrieving the ball; playing 'Follow my leader' in pairs; playing 'Robbers'. Games: making up a game of stopping and aiming the ball along the ground with a bat. Cool-down: running quickly in and out of the space.	● control a ball with a bat ● select appropriate equipment for the tasks set ● ensure fair turns when playing games
Can we improve our bat and ball skills?	● Run and change direction quickly. ● Practise catching individually and in pairs. ● Revise the underarm throw. ● Practise stopping and aiming a ball with a bat.	Warm-up: playing 'This way and that'; playing 'Side to side' and 'Shadows'. Development: rolling the ball for a partner to stop; trying slalom dribbling; striking the ball between two cones. Games: playing 'Piggy in the middle' along the floor. Cool-down: trying large and small steps to cross the space.	● respond to commands and change direction quickly ● control a ball with a bat ● are successful with their games
Can we aim and balance using bats and balls?	● Practise running with sudden changes of direction. ● Practise stopping and aiming the ball with the bat. ● Practise balancing and bouncing the ball with a bat. ● Make up a game of dribbling	Warm-up: jogging around the space; playing 'This way and that' and 'Side to side'. Development: balancing the ball on the bat, bouncing it and scooping it up again; following a partner, walking and balancing the ball on the bat; slalom dribbling. Games: making up a game of dribbling and passing in pairs. Cool-down: running on the spot fast and slow; hopping sideways.	● control a ball when dribbling in and out of cones

Enquiry questions	Learning objectives	Teaching activities	Learning outcomes
Can we combine our bat, balls and footwork skills?	● Try different ways of tap-bouncing a ball, with hand and bat. ● Practise footwork, quickly changing speed and direction, and begin dodging. ● Take turns with a partner to bounce a ball. ● Co-operate with a partner to beat own record.	Warm-up: jogging, changing direction; playing 'Chase the tail'. Development: practising tapping and bouncing the ball with a bat. Games: trying 'Pat-bouncing slalom' with a partner. Cool-down: bouncing and hitting back the ball in pairs.	● tap a ball in the air and keep it going, with control
How can we increase ball control?	● Practise footwork, quickly changing direction and dodging. Improve and practise bat and ball skills.	Warm-up: jogging in different directions; playing 'Chase the tail'. Development: bouncing the ball for a partner to catch, hit and return; rolling the ball to each other; tapping, bouncing and catching the ball over and under a net. Games: in pairs, one aiming for a target, other fielding. Cool-down: jogging, jumping then walking, following a partner.	● aim at a target ● dodge their partners.

Cross-curricular links
Maths: estimating distance.
PSHE: working together and co-operating.

Resources
Bats and a variety of small and medium balls – enough for one each; yellow and blue bands; photocopiable pages 158 and 159.

30 mins In what ways can we roll, tap and stop a ball?

**Learning
objectives**
● Practise bouncing
the ball and rolling
and tapping it
along the ground,
in different
directions, both for
accuracy and
distance.
● Practise different
ways of stopping
the ball with the
hands.
● Combine actions
of stopping a
rolling ball and
accurately
returning it to a
partner.
● Make up a game
of rolling, stopping
and aiming.

**Lesson
organisation**
Individual and
whole-class warm-
up; individual, then
paired activity;
paired cool-down;
teacher-led
classroom review.

What you need and preparation

Organise four colour-coded baskets of equipment and sufficient small or medium-sized balls for one ball each. You will also need yellow and blue bands; photocopiable page 158.

Organise the children into four colour-coded groups so they know which baskets to take their equipment from and return it to.

What to do

 Warm-up

Ask the children to run on the spot and then around the space, changing direction when you say *Change*. Tell them to weave in and out and use all directions. Practise stopping and starting.

Introduce the class to the game 'Jack Frost' (see photocopiable page 158). Choose four to six players to wear blue bands. These children are Jack Frost (the chasers). Choose a similar number of players to wear yellow bands (the sun). Explain that you want the rest of the children to run around the playground chased by Jack Frost. When children are caught they are frozen and have to stand still until they are released (touched on the arm) by the players with yellow bands (the sun) who can defrost them. Once thawed, the children can join in the game again and run around. Change over the children with bands until everyone has been either Jack Frost or the sun.

12 mins **Development**

Ask the children to collect a small or medium ball from the baskets and to practise bouncing it in a space. Help them to try several ways. Encourage them to try to beat their own record.

With the ball on the floor, ask them to practise tapping it around their feet (for example, through the legs, around both feet), without it rolling away. Encourage them to try several different ways – in different directions, stopping and starting, changing direction.

Tell the children now to keep the ball on the ground but to move it in any way they like around the space, keeping it close to them. They could choose to use their feet or hands or other variations. Encourage them to try this moving in different directions and to practise stopping and starting. Check that they are looking where they are going and are using the space well. Ask them to change and use another part of the body to move the ball (for example swap hands for feet).

When they have tried several ways, ask all the children to practise using the hand as a bat (flat and firm), this time moving the ball along the ground around the space. Let them practise, emphasising using lots of little taps and keeping the ball close to the hand.

Ask the children to make some patterns on the ground with the ball as they tap it (for example in a zigzag or curving pathway, making a triangle or other shape, following a line, writing their name and so on).

Encourage movement in different directions and stopping and starting by playing 'Change' – changing the direction of tapping on that command. Encourage the children to use their other hand, and emphasise the need to be aware of where they are going as well as looking at the ball.

Introduce and play the game 'Robbers'. Choose three or four children who, without a ball, move about the space looking for free balls. They are not allowed to touch or tackle but can take over and continue tapping any ball which is further than 50cm away from the player/tapper. Demonstrate how to do this if necessary.

Ask the children to find a partner and one of them to put one ball away. In pairs, with one ball between two, help them to stand facing each other, approximately 5m apart. Ask them to roll the ball backwards and forwards to their partner and to practise different ways of stopping the ball as it comes towards them.

Vocabulary
weaving in and out
Jack Frost
freeze
melt

Advise them to watch the ball and to crouch ready to stop the ball with their hands. Explain that they should be aiming for cupped hands with feet behind hands to act as a barrier. Ask them to repeat their attempts several times.

Challenge those who can do this easily by suggesting they move further apart or roll the ball more quickly. Encourage all pairs to count how many times they can roll the ball to each other without it going astray.

Challenge some children to roll the ball to the side of their partner so that their partner has to move to stop ball.

Now, ask the children to number themselves 1 and 2 and stand further apart. Ask them to practise retrieving and fielding. Explain that you want number 1 to hold the ball and be ready to roll it, slowly to begin with, into a big space while number 2 stands opposite them at the other side of the space, ready to receive the ball. Use demonstrations to emphasise aspects of fielding – moving their body into the pathway of a rolled ball, hands cupped to receive the ball, and so on. Encourage them to be alert and prepared to move in any direction, moving in line with the ball and putting hands and body behind the ball. When the children are doing this successfully, encourage them to vary the pace of the roll. Then swap over so everyone has tried rolling and fielding.

⏱ **Games**
10 mins Ask the children to make up a game which involves rolling the ball to their partner aiming at their hands or through their legs. Suggest number 1s stand with their backs to their partners and look through their legs to receive the ball. 2s then have the target of aiming and rolling the ball through the legs of their partners. Make sure that all the children have fair turns of aiming and receiving.

Encourage the children to combine actions of moving to receive, stopping and returning, by rolling the ball to a partner or a target.

Finally, let the pairs choose and try something they want to practise with the ball, with their partners or individually (collecting another ball if necessary).

Diagram 9

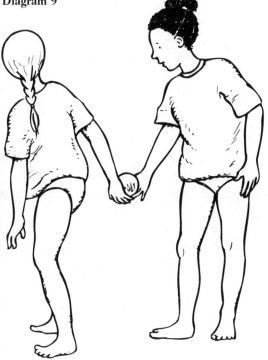

⏱ **Cool-down**
3 mins In pairs, ask the children to walk around the space, passing (not throwing) the ball to each other. Ask them to try different ways of passing and to move in different directions always looking for spaces.

In a space, ask them to pass the ball to their partners with two hands (through their legs over their heads, to the side and so on – see Diagram 9).

Classroom review
Encourage the children to describe their game to the rest of the class or to another group. Would they keep it the same if they played that game again next week?

Assessing learning outcomes
How well did the children stop, dribble and control the ball? Did they ensure fair turns in the games?

CHAPTER 3
GAMES

**Developing bat
and ball skills**

30 mins How can we use a bat?

**Learning
objectives**
● Practise different
ways of rolling and
stopping a ball.
● Practise tapping
and stopping a ball
with a bat.
● Practise dribbling
the ball in different
pathways.
● Make up a game
in twos, tapping,
stopping and
aiming the ball
along the ground
with a bat.

**Lesson
organisation**
Individual and
group warm-up;
individual then
paired activity;
individual cool-
down; teacher-led
classroom review.

Vocabulary
freeze
melt
tapping
stopping
aiming

What you need and preparation
You will need: baskets of equipment, placed on four sides of the play space, including a variety of
bats, balls, beanbags, rings skittles, blue and yellow bands; photocopiable page 158.

What to do

5 mins Warm-up
Ask the class to jog on the spot, then around the space, stopping and starting and changing
direction.

Remind the class how to play 'Jack Frost' (see photocopiable page 158). Again, make sure you
change the children who wear the bands until all the children have had a go at being either Jack
Frost or the sun.

15 mins Development
Ask the children to collect a small ball each and practise bouncing it in a space.

Ask them then to roll the ball into a space and to run after it as soon as it leaves their hand.
Encourage them to overtake the ball before stopping it and to turn to face the ball to stop it,
keeping their body behind the ball.

Now tell them to tap the ball along the ground with their hand, making different patterns or
shapes, using lots of little taps and keeping close to the ball. Challenge the more able children to
try this at varying speeds.

Ask everyone to collect a bat from the baskets and practise tapping the ball along the ground
around the playground space with their bat. Emphasise holding the bat firmly and using lots of
little taps, keeping the ball close to the bat. Encourage the children to stop and start and change
direction, and remind them to look where they are going now and again as well as looking at the
ball as much as they can.

Ask the children to make some patterns on the ground with the ball as they tap it, like they did
with their hands (in a zigzag or curving pathway, making a shape, writing their name and so on).

Play the game 'Change' by asking them to use their bat to stop or change direction with their
ball when you say *Change* or *Stop*. Encourage them to try using their bat with their other hand.

Next, play 'Robbers'. Choose three or four children who, without a ball, move about the space
looking for free balls as the rest of the class practise their pathways. Remind them that they are
not allowed to touch or tackle but can take over and continue tapping any ball which is further than
50cm away from the player/tapper.

Organise the children into pairs and introduce and play 'Follow my leader', one tapping the ball
around the space using different pathways, with their partner following and copying with their ball.

Then ask the children to stand a few metres apart from their partners (one bat each, one ball
between two). Explain that one player taps the ball for their partner to stop and then return. Ask
the children to try different ways of stopping the ball.

Now ask the pairs to try a variation on this. One player taps the ball *around* their partner and
back to their place. They then tap the ball to their partner who collects it to change over. Invite
them to practise this, then ask them if they can think of other ways to do this (such as going in the
other direction, using the other hand).

8 mins Games
Tell the children to keep in their pairs and make up a game of tapping, stopping and aiming
the ball along the ground with the bat. Encourage the pairs' efforts and ensure they are taking

turns. Ask them to choose two beanbags, rings or a skittle as a goal line or target to develop their game. Focus on stopping and aiming.

2 **Cool-down**
mins After the equipment has been put away, ask the children to spread out and find their own space, then run quickly in and out of the space, gradually slowing down. Encourage good use of different pathways (curved, zigzag and so on).

Classroom review
Encourage the children to reflect on the lesson. Ask them:
● How did you find stopping the ball with the bat?
● How did you have to hold the bat?
● What helped you aim towards your partner?

Assessing learning outcomes
Are the children able to control the ball with the bat? Are they able to select appropriate equipment for the tasks set (for example in making a target)? Do they ensure fair turns when playing the games?

30 Can we improve our bat and ball skills?
mins

What you need and preparation
You will need: four colour-coded baskets of equipment, including sufficient small balls and bats for one each; cones, beanbags or rings as markers; a whistle; photocopiable pages 158 and 159.
Organise the children into four colour-coded groups.

What to do
7 **Warm-up**
mins Ask the children to jog around the playground, using all the spaces. Encourage them to move in different directions, sideways and backwards as well as forwards, without touching each other. Tell them to listen out for your instructions as they move and to stop and start when you give the commands.

Next, ask all the children to face you in a space to play 'This way and that' (see photocopiable page 158). Point to your left and say *This way* and then point to your right and say *That way*. Alternate the instructions quickly to encourage sudden changes of direction. Encourage the children to catch up with anyone in front of them, but just as some begin to do so, reverse the instructions. Set some finishing lines well away from any fence or boundary.

Introduce the game 'Side to side' (see photocopiable page 159) to the class, in which the children practise sudden changes of direction, keeping up with a partner. Ask them to find a partner and to face each other in a big space, numbering themselves 1 and 2. Number 1s move from side to side and keep changing direction after a few steps, (sometimes one or two, sometimes three or four), suddenly stopping and starting. (Tell them not to run away!) Number 2s shadow their partner, trying to keep up with them and not letting them get more than two strides away. If, when you blow your whistle, they are close to their partner then they score a point. If their partner is more than two strides away then number 1 gets a point. Keep changing over the roles.

Alternatively, if it is sunny, introduce the children to 'Shadows' or 'Stand on your partner's head'. Number 1s move about the playground while 2s try to stand on the shadow of their partners' heads. Again, ensure everyone is taking fair turns.

Learning objectives
● Run and change direction quickly.
● Practise catching individually and in pairs.
● Revise the underarm throw.
● Practise stopping and aiming the ball with the bat.

Lesson organisation
Individual and paired warm-up and development; individual cool-down; teacher-led classroom review.

CHAPTER 3
G A M E S

**Developing bat
and ball skills**

Vocabulary
slalom
dribbling
estimate
guess
measure
shadow
stop
start
stride

(15 mins) Development

Ask the children to collect a ball each from the basket and to practise bouncing or tapping it in a space, counting how many times they can do that without letting the ball go astray. Encourage them to try to beat their own record. Tell them to try to remember their record for next time.

In pairs, with one ball between two, ask one child to roll the ball into a space for their partner to chase, collect and bring back, then roll back to the sender. Ask everyone to think of ways of taking turns (for example three goes each then change). Encourage them to help each other by pointing to the space where the ball is going.

Still in pairs (with one bat and one ball between two), ask the children to roll the ball gently for their partner to stop with their bat. Ask them to repeat this, trying to use different sides of the bat and standing in different positions and then to swap roles.

Ask the senders to roll the ball to the side of their partner. The partner should move to stop the ball with their bat.

Tell the children to get a ball and bat each and, in pairs, set up two cones or markers (use rubber rings or beanbags if necessary) for 'Follow my leader slalom dribbling'. Demonstrate if necessary and explain: one person follows their partner right around both markers in and out in a figure of eight. Ask the children to think of different ways they can do this (slowly, quickly, stopping and starting, using the other hand and so on).

Ask them to practise striking the ball to each other between the two cones, stopping the ball before returning it.

Diagram 10

(6 mins) Games

Organise the children into threes to play 'Piggy in the middle' (using two bats and one ball) with the ball on the floor (see Diagram 10). One player passes the ball to their partner using the bat and the third player tries to stop it. If 'piggy' touches the ball, they change places with the sender. It is important that the children are well spaced for this activity.

(2 mins) Cool-down

Ask everyone to move into a space. See if they can estimate then count how many large steps it takes for them to cross the playground. Invite them to repeat it to check.

Then ask them to estimate, then count, how many small steps it takes for them to cross between two lines.

Classroom review

Ask the children how the slalom dribbling went. *Would you change the circuit next time? What goals did you set up?*

Assessing learning outcomes

Were the children able to respond to commands and change direction quickly? How well did they control a ball with a bat? How successful were they with their games?

(30 mins) Can we aim and balance using bats and balls?

What you need and preparation

You will need: four baskets of colour-coded equipment, including sufficient bats and small balls for one each, cones, skittles and beanbags; a whistle; photocopiable pages 158 and 159.

Organise the children into four colour-coded groups.

What to do

(6 mins) Warm-up

Ask the children to jog around the playground using all the spaces. Encourage them to move in different directions, sideways and backwards as well as forwards, without touching each other. Ask them to listen and respond to your *Stop* and *Start* instructions.

Remind the children how to play 'This way and that' (see photocopiable page 158). Change your instructions frequently to encourage the children to make sudden changes of direction. Remind the children to try to catch up with anyone in front of them, but just as they begin to do so, reverse your instructions again. Set some finishing lines well away from any fence or boundary.

Organise the children into pairs and play the game 'Side to side' to help the children to practise sudden changes of direction and keeping up with a partner (see photocopiable page 159). Remind the pairs that you want one of them to move from side to side and keep changing direction after a few steps, suddenly stopping and starting, and that their partner is to shadow them, trying to keep up with them and not letting them get more than two strides away. Tell the chasers that if they are close to their partner when you blow your whistle, they score a point, but if their partner is more than two strides away then *they* get a point. Make sure they keep changing over so everyone has had a few turns at shadowing and 'escaping'.

(15 mins) Development

Ask all the children to collect a ball and a bat from the basket and to practise bouncing or tapping it in a space. Ask: *Can you beat your record?* Tell them to count how many times they can tap the ball without letting it go astray. Encourage them to try several times.

Ask the children to try balancing the ball on the bat held out in front of them. Tell them to try walking around the playground, seeing if they can keep it on the bat. If it slides off, suggest they try to scoop it back up again with the bat. Remind them to look where they are going as they manoeuvre in and out of each other.

Encourage everyone to think of ways they can make this a bit more difficult. For example, moving faster, moving in different directions, changing positions (crouching, turning around). Challenge more able children to try jogging or walking backwards when doing this. Ask them all to try using their other hand.

In pairs, ask the children to try to follow a partner, walking and balancing the ball on the bat. See if they can copy their partner's actions and then tell them to change leaders.

Play 'Slalom dribbling'. In pairs, ask the children to choose two cones or markers (such as rings) and practise 'Follow my leader' in different pathways in and out or round both markers, balancing the ball on the bat. Ask them to vary the speed of the movement.

With their partners, can the children think of and try other actions that they could do while balancing the ball on the bat? (For example crouching down or turning around.)

(6 mins) Games

Ask the children, in their pairs, to make up a game of dribbling and passing, with two bats and one ball. Ask them to set up two markers like a goal and to stand one each side of the goal.

Learning objectives
● Practise running with sudden changes of direction.
● Practise stopping and aiming the ball with the bat.
● Practise balancing and bouncing the ball with a bat.
● Make up a game of dribbling and passing in pairs.

Lesson organisation
Individual and paired warm-up; individual then paired games; individual cool-down; teacher-led classroom review.

Vocabulary
bouncing
balancing
slalom dribbling

Advise them to co-operate in passing the ball to each other through the goal. Ask them to count how many times they can do this.

- Can you beat your record?
- What helps you to be accurate?
- What do you need to do?

Encourage a good follow-through in the direction of the pass and to watch the ball as it leaves their partner's bat.

(3 mins) Cool-down

Ask the children to run quickly into a space and then run on the spot, fast and slow, fast and slow. Ask them to hop sideways for five hops and then hop back to their place.

Classroom review

Ask the children how their game worked out – was it successful? What could they do to make it easier or more difficult?

Assessing learning outcomes

Could the children control the ball when dribbling in and out of the cones?

(30 mins) Can we combine our bat, ball and footwork skills?

What you need and preparation

You will need: four baskets of colour-coded equipment, including sufficient bats and small balls for one each, bands, cones, skittles and beanbags; photocopiable page 159.

Organise the children into four colour-coded groups.

What to do

(5 mins) Warm-up

Ask the children to jog around the playground using all the spaces. Encourage them to move in lots of directions, swerving in and out of each other without touching. Tell them to gradually increase the speed to a running action and change direction when you say *Change* or stop altogether when you say *Stop*.

Play 'Chase the tail' (see photocopiable page 159). Ask the children to find a partner and label themselves 'A' and 'B'. Ask the 'A's to collect a band from their basket and tuck it into the back of their shorts (see Diagram 11). When you say *Go*, the 'B's try to pull the 'tail' out. Advise the 'A's to try to keep facing their partner. Change over when the band is caught or to ensure fair turns.

(12 mins) Development

Individually, ask the children to collect a ball and a bat and practise bouncing the ball in a space. Then ask them to practise tapping the ball up in the air, letting it bounce and tapping it up again. Ask them to repeat this several times, trying to beat their record number of taps without it

Diagram 11

bouncing more than twice. Encourage them to watch the ball and to try to get the bat underneath it to tap it upwards rather than forwards.

If a suitable wall is available, ask the children to tap their ball against it, letting the ball bounce and tapping it back. Help them to take it in turns if space is limited.

In pairs, tell the children to collect four markers (cones, beanbags or skittles). Ask them to lay them out in a space and practise bouncing the ball in and out of them with their bat. Then help them to play 'Pat-bouncing slalom'. Nominate one partner as the leader, the other as the follower. The followers must follow their partners in a course around the markers. Tell them to move the markers and repeat the exercise. The markers could be further apart or closer together, as each pair chooses. Ensure that everyone has the chance to be both a leader and a follower.

10 mins Games

In their pairs, ask the children to play 'Pat-bouncing' (or to make up a game of their own). In this game, the pairs take it in turns to bounce the ball towards their partner who then continues the bouncing, back to the position that the first child started from.

To finish with, ask the pairs to put one bat away. Using one bat and one ball, ask one player to bounce the ball for their partner to hit back for them to catch. Emphasise that this is a co-operative activity. Suggest five goes each and ask the children to count how many they can catch in a row. Emphasise careful aiming by the senders.

3 mins Cool-down

Still in pairs, ask the children to walk around the space, one following the other, keeping close. Tell them to take turns to lead, using interesting pathways. Encourage them then to slow down gradually to slow-motion walking.

Classroom review

Ask the children which was easier – tapping the ball on the ground or tapping it in the air? Ask them how well they co-operated with their partner.

Assessing learning outcomes

Could the children tap the ball in the air and keep it going? Could they do this with control?

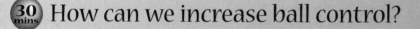

30 mins How can we increase ball control?

What you need and preparation

You will need: four baskets of colour-coded equipment including sufficient bats and small balls for one each, bands, cones, skittles, beanbags; photocopiable page 159.

Organise the children into four colour-coded groups.

What to do

5 mins Warm-up

Ask the children to sidestep around the playground using all the spaces. Encourage them to use both directions. Then ask them to jog around, swerving in and out of each other without touching. Gradually increase the speed to a running action, asking them to change direction or stop when you give the appropriate instruction.

Ask everyone to find a partner and label themselves 'A' and 'B' ready to play 'Chase the tail' (see photocopiable page 159). Remind the 'A's to try to keep their tails away from their partners. Tell the children to swap roles when the band is caught or as appropriate to ensure fair turns.

Learning objectives
● Practise footwork, quickly changing direction and dodging.
● Improve and practise bat and ball skills.

Lesson organisation
Individual and paired warm-up; paired practise and games; paired cool-down; teacher-led classroom review.

Developing bat and ball skills

Development

12 mins With a bat and a ball each, ask the children individually to practise the bat and ball skills they have tried over the past few weeks. Can they try to beat their own record at consecutive bounces, tapping up and so on?

Then, in pairs, ask them to set up a goal using two cones or markers, and to practise bouncing the ball downwards, taking it in turns to follow each other through and around the goal (in and out of the cones).

Ask the pairs to put one ball away and to take it in turns to practise aiming and passing through the markers to each other, stopping the ball with the bat. Can they co-operatively count how many times they can do this without the ball going astray? Challenge more able children to pass through the cones at different angles, anticipating the path of the ball. Ask one member of the pair to tap the ball while their partner watches it, then stops and returns it, aiming through the cones at an angle for the origindal sender to receive. Ensure everyone takes fair turns.

This time, with one ball and one bat between two, ask one player from each pair to bounce the ball between the cones for their partner to return, hitting it back for the first sender to catch. How many can their partner catch?

Games

10 mins With one bat and one ball between two, ask each pair to set up a target (for example a mark on the wall or between two cones). Explain that one is to aim and send while the other fields. Help the sender to get into a position to strike the ball at the target. Tell the fielder to watch the ball as it comes back from (or goes through) the target. Ask them to collect the ball and roll it back to the sender who repeats the challenge four times before they change roles. Encourage the partners to keep score for each other.

Ask the pairs to make up and practise their own game with two bats and one ball.

Cool-down

3 mins With a partner, ask the children to jog, jump then walk around the space, one following the other, keeping close. Tell them to take turns to lead, and to use interesting pathways.

Classroom review

Ask the children to discuss how they helped each other in their games. What did they enjoy doing the most?

Assessing learning outcomes

How successful were the children in aiming at the target? Did they manage to dodge their partners?

CHAPTER 4

Swimming

For those of us who have been privileged to share a child's delight in accomplishing those first few swimming strokes unaided, there is little need to extol the virtues and benefits of swimming as an educational activity. In today's world, competence and confidence in this medium are essential for safety and survival.

Swimming provides an excellent form of relaxation or challenging exercise, and also opens access to a variety of other exciting water sports like sailing, canoeing and windsurfing. Water has many attractions and can provide an important medium for learning, not just how to swim, but also about health and fitness, safety and the environment. Similarly, the swimming pool can provide first-hand experience of the effect of water on the body, and a variety of scientific principles like those relating to flotation, propulsion and resistance.

Although we know that swimming is important for safety, survival, confidence, fitness and recreation, it is very unlikely (unless the school has its own learner pool) that classes will be taken swimming for more than a short time during a child's primary schooling. Teaching swimming, therefore, will be unique to each school and very dependent upon facilities available, authority guidelines, staffing and expertise available, any previous experience of the children, timetabling, transport, funds, and many other factors.

Schools can choose to teach swimming during Key Stage 1. Although it is non-statutory, the National Curriculum recommends that 'pupils should be taught to swim unaided for a sustained period of time over a distance of at least 25 metres' by the end of Key Stage 2, and demonstrate an understanding of water safety. Your school will need to decide how the National Curriculum requirements are met. Some children will be confident and competent swimmers, while others may be quite fearful of the water and find the pool an intimidating or frightening experience.

For the purposes of this book, some limited guidelines are offered for the teacher accompanying their class to a pool, and a unit of work is included for teachers helping a small group of beginners.

The ideas are intended to help make moving in water and learning to swim an enjoyable and safe learning experience for children who may be new to this environment.

For young children, it is helpful if a number of parents or other helpers/assistants are invited to be involved to help children in the changing rooms. Grouping will need to be considered carefully by or with the instructor. Whatever the organisation, try to keep the children active so they do not get cold.

There are several health and safety requirements that apply particularly to swimming. Children should be taught about hazards, risks and risk control, and to manage their environment to ensure the safety of themselves and others. To these must be added:
- to respond readily to instructions
- to follow the relevant rules and safety procedures
- to understand and implement aspects of hygiene.

Guidelines for accompanying your class to a pool

Prepare the children and inform the parents well before the lessons take place:
- Talk to them about swimming.
- Explain arrangements for getting to the pool.
- Discuss what to expect (the depth of the pool, the noise level), and what to bring (a bag for wet clothing, swimming cap).
- Describe changing procedures (where to go, where the toilets are).
- Explain hygiene requirements (for example blowing noses, showering, using footbaths).
- Discuss how to take care of dry clothes (the use of lockers).
- Talk about the use of swimming aids.

For all beginners, the use of armbands or other well-fitting buoyancy aids can help to provide the much-needed confidence to start floating and moving in water.

Alert the swimming instructor to any medical conditions (ear infections and so on) or physical impairments and discuss any special arrangements needed, such as having asthma inhalers by the poolside. To include all children (for example those with a physical impairment), you may need to find out if hoists are available and if a helper is needed for one-to-one support.

Help to familiarise your class with the environment (the shallow and deep ends of the water, if appropriate, changing rooms and toilets, the fire exit and so on).

Discuss water safety principles in the classroom beforehand. Children will need to follow specific rules and safety procedures. Discuss safety and the pool's code of practice and ask the children to think about why some rules are necessary (for example *Walk, don't run; No shouting, jumping or pushing* and so on).

The children will need to follow general and specific hygiene requirements (visiting the toilets, blowing their noses, having a foot check, using the footbaths and so on). Safety and hygiene in different environments are important parts of the general requirement of health and relate particularly to the welfare of school children.

Children will need to know how to respond to instructions in this environment and why it is so important to listen out for and expect them. (Because of the high noise level and water in their ears.) Insist on them listening and watching. Establish a routine for waiting – sitting before being told to get into the pool. Establish and check procedures for gaining their attention and stopping the whole class (perhaps using a whistle and/or hand signals).

Encourage and support the children with your interest in their efforts and their progress.

Above all, always ensure that you are in a position where you can see *all* the children and observe their efforts and responses.

Developing confidence in the water

This series of lessons is unlike others in this book, as it is designed for a group of children who are being introduced to this PE environment – water – for the first time, in a learner or beginners' pool. (As a general rule, non-swimmers should be at least 15–25cm taller than the depth of water they are expected to use.)

All the activities are designed to help children feel 'at home' in the water and to gradually build up their confidence in moving about in the pool. It will incorporate a number of games, which it is hoped they will enjoy, to take their minds off possible fears. Play in water can be an enjoyable way of learning and practising skills, but must be carefully matched to the confidence of the children involved. Children will need varying levels of support from swimming aids.

The unit is non-statutory, but it is always recommended that children learn to swim at the earliest opportunity.

The children will have had very different experiences of water and some may not have been to a pool before, so talk to them well in advance of the sessions. Help to prepare them for what to expect, and establish what they should know before they go to or get into the pool:

- what to bring and what to wear
- the changing routine
- the pool layout.

Safety procedures

Make sure that the children are fully aware of all health and safety procedures, including:

- hygiene – using the toilet, blowing their noses, taking a shower or footbath
- the stopping procedure
- how to use swimming and buoyancy aids.

Organisation

Ensure that there is adequate supervision in the changing rooms for young children; it is helpful if a number of parents are invited to assist with the journey and with changing.

Keep the children active so that they do not get cold.

The timings of the lessons will generally be about 20–30 minutes, but will depend very much on group sizes and individual circumstances.

UNIT: Developing confidence in the water

Enquiry questions	Learning objectives	Teaching activities	Learning outcomes
How can we get used to the water?	●Get in and out of the pool using steps. ●Walk along the side of the pool, introducing a pulling action with one arm or two. ●Orientate in the water. ●Get shoulders under the water. ●Bob up and down, bringing knees to chest. ●Blow bubbles. ●Play in the water.	Introduction and development: getting in and out of the pool using the steps; walking along the side of the pool, introducing a pulling action with one arm or two; orientating in the water (moving to the left or right, turning round); getting shoulders under the water and rubbing parts of the body with water; bobbing up and down, bringing knees to chest; breathing – blowing bubbles; playing 'Jack in the box'. Games: playing 'What's the time, Mr Shark?'	Children: ●gain confidence in the water ●leave the side of the pool ●get their faces near the water
How can we begin to move in the water?	●Slip into the water from the side. ●Walk along the side of the pool, developing pulling actions with arms. ●Get shoulders under the water and bring knees to chest. ●Kick and reach for the side of the pool. ●Blow bubbles. ●Play with a ball in the water.	Introduction and development: slipping into the water from the side; walking along the side of the pool, developing the pulling action with arms; getting shoulders under the water and bringing knees to chest; kicking with the legs and reach for the side of the pool; breathing – blowing bubbles. Games: playing with a ball in the water and 'What's the time, Mr Shark?'	●regain their feet ●breathe near or in the water ●kick well, with long legs
How can we move about in the water?	●Practise getting in from the side. ●Try to walk without holding on to the rail. ●Breathe close to the water. ●Develop the horizontal streamlined position, bending knees to regain standing position. ●Practise wading and pulling actions. ●Develop a kicking action.	Introduction and development: practising getting in from the side; trying to walk without holding on to the rail; playing 'Follow my leader'; breathing close to the water; developing the horizontal streamlined position, bending knees to regain standing position; practising wading and pulling arm action; kicking and gliding. Games: playing 'Boats'; practising with a ball; playing 'Ring-a-ring o' roses'.	●begin to show more confidence in the water ●move around the pool without always holding on to the sides
What can we do with floats?	●Practise getting in from the side. ●Blow bubbles close to the water. ●Practise bending knees to regain a standing position. ●Practise the horizontal position while kicking. ●Jump while in the water. ●Pass a ball.	Introduction and development: practising getting in from the side; breathing – blowing bubbles close to or under the water; practising bending knees to regain a standing position; practising the horizontal position while kicking; jumping while in the water, holding on to the side with both hands, one hand or not at all. Games: playing 'Simon says' and 'Ring-a-ring o' roses'.	●begin to adopt a more horizontal position in the water

Enquiry questions	Learning objectives	Teaching activities	Learning outcomes
How can we gain confidence in the water?	● Practise the long, horizontal position while kicking. ● Practise blowing bubbles along or under the surface of the water. ● Practise using a float.	Introduction and development: playing 'This way and that'; practising the long, horizontal position while kicking; breathing – blowing bubbles along or under the surface of the water; blowing table tennis balls across the surface of the pool; practising kicking while using a float. Games: playing 'Simon says' and 'Oranges and lemons'.	● adopt a more horizontal position in the water ● breathe under or near the surface of the water
What can we do to develop greater confidence in the water?	● Use a float and kick with long legs. ● Blow table tennis balls across the surface of the pool.	Introduction and development: playing 'This way and that'; practise turning around without touching the bottom; walking with shoulders under water; using a float while kicking to travel across the pool; blowing bubbles under the water; blowing a table tennis ball across the water. Games: playing 'Blow football'; 'Simon says' or 'Oranges and lemons'.	● combine the breathing and leg-kick actions ● increase their confidence ● are more comfortable and enjoy being in the water.

Cross-curricular links
Science: learning about why things float and sink.
PSHE: being aware of health and hygiene.

Resources
Floats; armbands; light plastic balls of different sizes.

Developing confidence in the water

30 mins How can we get used to the water?

Learning objectives
● Get in and out of the pool using the steps.
● Walk along the side of the pool, introducing a pulling action with one arm or two.
● Orientate in the water.
● Get shoulders under the water.
● Bob up and down, bringing knees to chest.
● Blow bubbles.
● Play in the water.
● Play 'What's the time, Mr Shark?'

Lesson organisation
Classroom discussion about swimming; individual, paired and whole-class exercises under close supervision.

What you need and preparation
Floats should be provided at the pool. Provide armbands as appropriate.

In the classroom, talk to the children about swimming. Discuss their previous experiences.
● Have they been to a swimming pool before?
● Have they swum in the sea?
● What do they like and dislike about water?
● What does the water feel like to move around in?
● What can they do or play in the water?
● What can be heard in the pool?

What to do

20 mins Introduction and development
At the pool, ask the children to line up in single file and to walk carefully to the edge of the pool and sit down on the side. Encourage them to put their feet in the water and to stretch their toes. When everyone is doing this, encourage them to shake their ankles and then to point their toes and *gently* splash their feet.

Ask them to stand, line up again and walk to the steps. One at a time, encourage them to climb down the steps with their backs to the water until their feet are on the bottom of the pool. When they are in the water, ask them to hold the rail with both hands and to slide their feet sideways along the bottom as they walk, holding on to the rail.

Ask them to walk along the side, holding on to the rail with both hands, then with just one hand. Practise turning around, holding on with one hand, to walk back again.

Repeat the walking exercise, but this time ask the children to reach and pull with their free hand as they walk along. Encourage those who want to try to do so with both hands. Encourage the children who feel confident to take a step away from the rail and to walk back to their original position without holding on.

Ask the children to bend their knees to get their shoulders under the water and to practise bobbing up and down. Make this fun by encouraging them to watch each other in pairs: one bobs down as the other one comes up.

Now tell everyone to scoop some water in their hands and to 'wash' their shoulders, then to choose some other parts to wash (perhaps including their ears and noses). Encourage them to wash their faces and to blow the water off their hands. See if they can blow bubbles in the water, in their hands or on the surface of the water (see Diagram 1).

Play 'Jack in the box': encouraging the children to get a bit lower in the water before they pop up or jump upwards. Some children will want to hold on to the side doing this, while others might be able to do it independently. Advise them all to keep their feet apart for stability and to try changing the position of their feet in the water (such as one foot forward and one back or side by side).

Diagram 1

Vocabulary
breathing
blowing bubbles
turning
shake
stretch
splash
bobbing
shark

**Developing confidence
in the water**

Ask the children to hold on to the side of the pool and encourage them to lift one foot or both feet off the bottom, tucking their knees to their chest if they can. See if some can try this holding their arms outstretched, without holding on to the side.

Ask everyone to hold on to the rail and to stretch out, moving their feet further away from the side. Ask them to raise one leg behind them, then the other one so that their bodies are more or less horizontal. Teach them to bend their knees to regain the standing position, bringing their knees to their chest or their chin and then pushing down with the heels to stand (see Diagram 2). Watch as they practise this several times.

Diagram 2

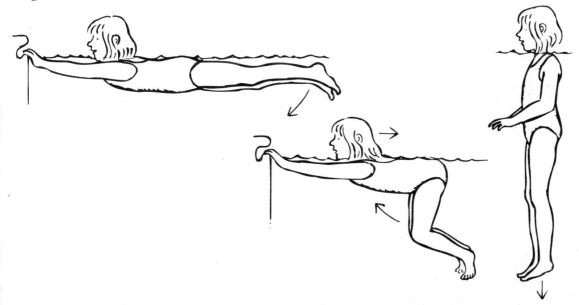

Help and encourage the children to get into a horizontal streamlined position, holding on to the rail, and see if they can start to kick with both legs (see Diagram 3). Ask them to have a go at kicking their legs in a few different ways.

Diagram 3

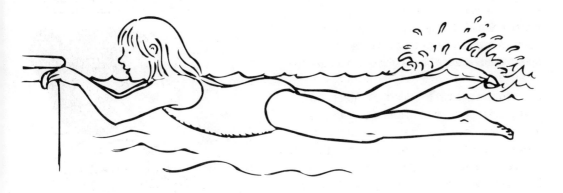

Developing confidence
in the water

10 **Games**
mins Play 'Follow my leader' in pairs, one leading (walking, wading, turning around and so on), the other following their route and their actions.

Allow some time for free practise so that the children can show you what they can do in the water. Then play 'What's the time, Mr Shark?' Explain the game to the children. One confident child (the shark) stands towards the middle of the pool (make sure the whole area is of the same depth) and turns their back away from the group. The others try to creep up on the shark to touch them. If the shark turns around, everyone has to freeze. If the shark spots someone moving, that child goes back to the side of the pool to start again.

Assessing learning outcomes
How confident are the children in the water? Who is able to leave the side of the pool? Can they get their faces near the water?

30 How can we begin to move in the water?
mins

Learning objectives
● Slip into the water from the side.
● Walk along the side of the pool, developing pulling actions with arms.
● Get shoulders under the water and bring knees to chest.
● Kick and reach for the side of the pool.
● Blow bubbles.
● Play with a ball in the water.

Lesson organisation
Classroom discussion about swimming; individual, paired and whole-class exercises under close supervision.

Vocabulary
reaching
pulling
kicking

What you need and preparation
You will need: light plastic balls of different sizes, enough for one between two; floats and armbands as appropriate.

In the classroom, talk about what it felt like to be in the water.

What to do
20 **Introduction and development**
mins Ask the children to sit on the side of the pool and to move their bottoms towards the edge. Show them how to put their hands on the side or on the rail to take their weight on their arms and slip gently into the water, still holding on to the side of the pool (see Diagram 4).

Ask them to practise sliding their feet, then walking along holding on to the side of the pool with one hand or, if possible, letting go for some of the time.

With the children facing you and the rail, ask them to cup their hands and to scoop up some water. Encourage them to bring this up towards their face and to blow the water off. Let them practise this a few times. Then encourage them to wash their faces in the water, or to just put their chins on the water. Some of them may be able to splash their faces or blow bubbles under the water.

Encourage all the children to practise bobbing up and down in the water to get their shoulders wet and to start them moving. Tell them to practise this again, this time in pairs, one going down as the other one bobs up.

Individually, see if they can keep their shoulders under the water and lift their knees to their chests before putting their feet on the bottom.

Diagram 4

With their shoulders under the water, ask the children to walk, then wade, gradually making bigger strides, and then to practise reaching out and pulling with their arms. Some may be able to do this without holding on. Encourage all the children to keep low in the water and remind them to pull with both arms.

Next, ask them to practise holding on to the sides and kicking with long legs. Encourage them to kick with their feet up to the surface.

Ask the children to find a partner each and to walk in pairs, holding hands. Ask them then to try walking one behind the other, holding on to the front person's shoulders. Tell them to change leaders and practise.

Games

10 mins Give the pairs one ball between two, and suggest that they pass the ball to their partner in as many different ways as they can.

Allow some time for free practise so that children can show you what they can do in the water. Then finish by playing 'What's the time, Mr Shark?'

Assessing learning outcomes
Do the children regain their feet easily? Can they breathe near the water? How well do they kick?

30 mins How can we move about in the water?

What you need and preparation
You will need: enough light plastic balls of different sizes, for one between two; floats and armbands.

In the classroom, talk to the children about the temperature of the water, how it makes them feel and what they can do to feel warmer in the water.

What to do
20 mins Introduction and development
Ask the children to practise getting in from the side. They could do this several times, walking back to the steps or climbing to get out again. Those who are confident sliding in could try turning to the other side to slide in.

Ask everyone to try walking, holding on to the rail and then to try it without holding on, keeping their shoulders under the water, with big steps or little steps, moving sideways, using their arms to reach and pull.

Remind the children how to play 'Follow my leader', and ask them, in pairs, to follow a partner's course and actions.

Then, individually, tell them to practise breathing close to the water and blowing bubbles.

Ask all the children to practise standing away from the rail and turning around in the water, using their arms to help. Encourage them to have a go in both directions.

Next, ask them to hold on to the side and try to run in the water. Ask them to try this quickly and in slow motion running, lifting their feet a bit more off the bottom of the pool. Tell them to practise wading through the water, using their arms to pull the water towards them. Encourage them to use their arms alternately or try using both at the same time. Encourage each child to do this at their own level, as best they can.

Ask everyone to take up a horizontal streamlined position, holding on to the rail, and teach them to bend their knees to regain the standing position. Practise this together several times. Then ask them to hold on to the rail and try kicking their legs, keeping them as stretched and as long as they can. Advise them to vary the speed of their kicks.

Learning objectives
● Practise getting in from the side.
● Try to walk without holding on to the rail.
● Breathe close to the water.
● Develop the horizontal streamlined position, bending knees to regain standing position.
● Practise wading and pulling actions.
● Develop a kicking action.

Lesson organisation
Classroom discussion; individual, paired and small-group exercises under close supervision.

**Developing confidence
in the water**

Vocabulary
horizontal
streamlined
glide

Now get everyone together, standing facing the rail, a step away from the side of the pool. With their shoulders under the water and with one foot in front of the other, encourage them to push with their back foot and reach out towards the side of the pool. Encourage them to glide smoothly rather than lurch and to lift both legs off the bottom (see Diagram 5). Encourage them to practise this and to start a step further away if they can.

Suggest playing 'Boats' in pairs, with one child walking forwards, pulling with their hands and the other one holding on to them, kicking with their legs.

Diagram 5

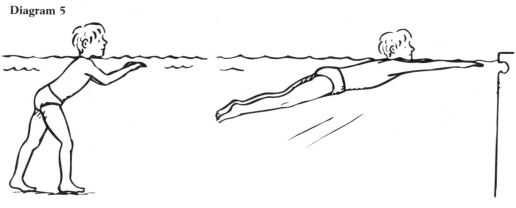

 Games

Allow some time for free practise so that the children can show you individually what they can do in the water. Then, with one ball between two, ask them to practise passing and receiving the ball with their partner.

Ask the children to get into groups of four, holding hands in a circle ready to play 'Ring-a-ring o' roses'. Sing the rhyme together a few times, asking the children to walk in one direction, and on *Atishoo, atishoo*, ask them to shake their bodies. On *all fall down*, ask them to bob down in the water. Encourage them to get a bit lower in the water each time they 'all fall down'.

Assessing learning outcomes
Are the children beginning to show more confidence in the water? Can they move around the pool without always holding on to the sides?

30 mins What can we do with floats?

Learning objectives
• Practise getting in from the side.
• Blow bubbles close to the water.
• Practise bending knees to regain standing position.
• Practise the horizontal position while kicking.
• Jump while in the water.
• Pass a ball.

What you need and preparation
You will need: sufficient floats for one or two per child; one table tennis ball each; armbands.

In the classroom, talk to the children about the safety rules in the pool (for example *No running*), and why they are important.

What to do
20 mins Introduction and development
First of all, encourage the children to practise getting in from the side several times, walking back to the steps or climbing to get out again. Encourage those who are doing well at sliding in to try turning to the other side to do so.

Invite everyone to practise wading and walking along the side of the pool, holding on or not, depending on their confidence. Then ask them to pull themselves along the side, trying to keep their feet off the bottom.

Developing confidence in the water

Now help the children to practise their breathing, asking them to blow bubbles close to or under the surface of the water. Encourage them to practise blowing bubbles on every out breath (see Diagram 6).

Use table tennis balls to aid this, and encourage the children to practise in pairs (taking it in turns, having races or playing blow football).

Lesson organisation
Brief classroom discussion; individual, paired and whole-class exercises under close supervision.

Diagram 6

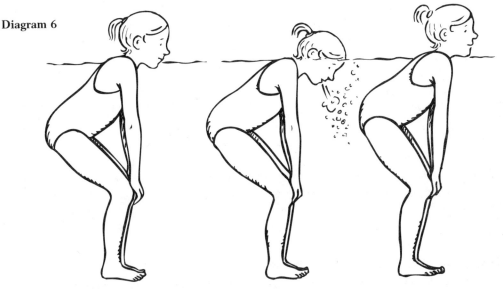

Ask everyone to practise the horizontal streamlined position and to practise lifting and bending their knees to regain the standing position.

Help the children to link together a sequence of kicking and then regaining a standing position several times. While they are kicking, emphasise long legs with movement from the hips.

Encourage them to practise reaching out and gliding towards the side, starting with their shoulders under the water. See if they can practise doing this smoothly, and from further back each time.

Briefly introduce floats, teaching the children to hold the float firmly out in front of them (see Diagram 8 on page 140). Then encourage them to rest *on* their floats to glide and kick, starting with their shoulders under the water.

Collect in the floats and ask the children to jump up and down in the water, holding on to the side with both hands, then with one hand, then, if they feel confident enough, without holding on at all. Encourage them to vary the position of their feet.

Ask the children to get their shoulders under the water and see if they can briefly kneel or even sit down on the bottom of the pool.

In pairs, ask them to hold hands facing each other and to number themselves 1 and 2. Explain that you want 1s to keep their feet firmly on the ground and 2s to jump their feet off the bottom of the pool, holding on to their partner's hands. Ensure that they take fair turns.

Vocabulary
horizontal streamlined reach and glide wading

(10 mins) Games

Introduce 'Simon says', suggesting actions that have been covered in previous sessions (including bobbing up and down, kicking their legs out while holding on to the side and so on).

Allow some free practise time for the children to show you what they can do in the water. Finish with a game of 'Ring-a-ring o' roses' (see page 138) and then the children's choice of game.

Assessing learning outcomes

Are the children beginning to adopt a more horizontal position in the water?

30 mins How can we gain confidence in the water?

Learning objectives
● Practise the long, horizontal position while kicking.
● Blow bubbles along or under the surface of the water.
● Practise using a float.

Lesson organisation
Classroom discussion about swimming; individual, paired and whole-class exercises under close supervision.

Vocabulary
horizontal streamlined position

What you need and preparation

You will need: enough floats for one or two per child; one table tennis ball each; armbands as appropriate.

In the classroom before going to the pool, recap with the children the importance of the horizontal streamlined position.

What to do

20 mins Introduction and development

Play 'This way and that' by asking the children to face you in a space in the water. Those who are less confident can be nearer the rail. Explain that when you say *This way* and point to your right, they should move in that direction, and when you say *That way* and point to your left, they move that way. Encourage them to pull with their arms to help them move through the water.

Ask everyone to practise the long, horizontal streamlined position while kicking with long legs. Ask them to keep kicking while you count to five or ten and so on. Organise the children into pairs and ask one person from each pair to kick first, while their partner watches, and then to swap over. Let them practise this several times.

Now ask all the children to get their shoulders under the water and to breathe as close to the water as they can. Encourage them to blow bubbles on the out breath. Advise them to take a deep breath in and blow the out breath under the water.

Invite them to practise their breathing by blowing table tennis balls across the surface of the pool (see Diagram 7).

After a short while, hand out a float to each child. Back in their pairs, tell one child to watch as their partner holds the float

Diagram 7

firmly out in front of them and tries to kick across to the other side of the pool. Again, make sure they swap over so everyone has several practices. NB. Some children who lack confidence may prefer two floats. Demonstrate how to hold them correctly, with their arms extended (see Diagram 8).

Diagram 8

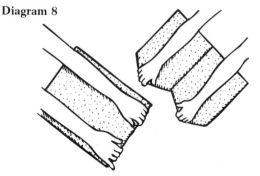

10 mins Games

Allow some free practise then play 'Simon says' or 'Oranges and lemons'. Ask two children to make an arch and the others to wade or swim through the arch in a line while they sing the rhyme. At the end of the rhyme, the arch is lowered suddenly and the child who is caught changes places with one of those making the arch.

Assessing learning outcomes

Can the children adopt a more horizontal position in the water? Can they breathe under or near the surface of the water?

Developing confidence
in the water

(30 mins) What can we do to develop greater confidence in the water?

What you need and preparation

You will need: enough floats for one or two per child; one table tennis ball each; armbands as appropriate.

In the classroom, talk to the children about the horizontal streamlined position.

What to do

(20 mins) Introduction and development

Ask the children to slide into the pool, remind them of previous practises.

When they are settled, play 'This way and that' (see page 140). Encourage them to pull with their arms to help them move through the water.

Then ask them to practise turning around in the water, without their feet touching the bottom if they can.

Next, encourage them to walk slowly backwards in the water. See if they can put their shoulders under the water, and remind them to be aware of where they are going. Emphasise that they should be sculling their hands as they are walking.

Gather everyone to face you at the side of the pool and ask them to practise kicking while holding on to the rail. Encourage them to speed up and then slow down the rate of their kicks.

Hand out the floats and tell the children to hold their float out in front of them. Encourage them to kick with long legs to move in the water and get across to the other side of the pool. Help them understand why they need to keep the body horizontal and streamlined – to reduce resistance from the water. Afterwards, encourage those who feel confident enough to try letting themselves lie fairly still and feel the water support them.

Ask everyone to practise blowing bubbles along and under the surface of the water. Encourage them to do this with a regular rhythm (lifting their heads to breathe in then blowing out under the surface of the water). Then, holding on to the rail or their floats, see if the children can link the breathing with the leg kick.

With a table tennis ball each, ask them to blow the ball across the surface of the pool. After several practises, suggest that they get into pairs and make a race of this with their partner.

(10 mins) Games

Tell the children to keep in their pairs and continue playing with the table tennis ball; this time a game of blow football.

Allow some time for free practise so that the children can show you what they can do in the water. Finish by playing 'Simon says' or 'Oranges and lemons'.

Assessing learning outcomes

Are the children able to combine the breathing and leg kick actions? Has their confidence increased? Are they more comfortable and starting to enjoy being in the water?

Learning objectives
● Use a float and kick with long legs.
● Blow table tennis balls across the surface of the pool.
● Develop confidence in moving and playing in the water.
● Practise rhythmic breathing.

Lesson organisation
Classroom discussion; individual introduction and development; paired and whole-class games under close supervision.

Vocabulary
sculling
this way and that

'J' action words

jump

jog

jerk

jiggle

jagged

'C' action words

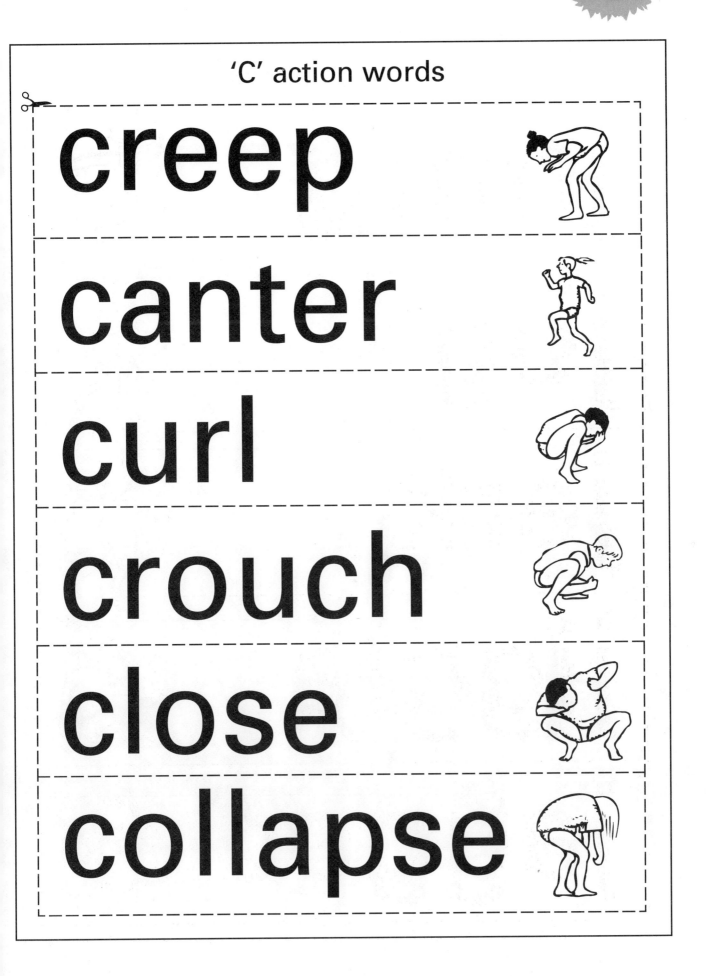

creep

canter

curl

crouch

close

collapse

'D' action words

dance

dart

drift

drop

'T' action words

tiptoe

twist

turn

tremble

thin

'W' action words

walk

wander

wobble

whirl

'S' action words

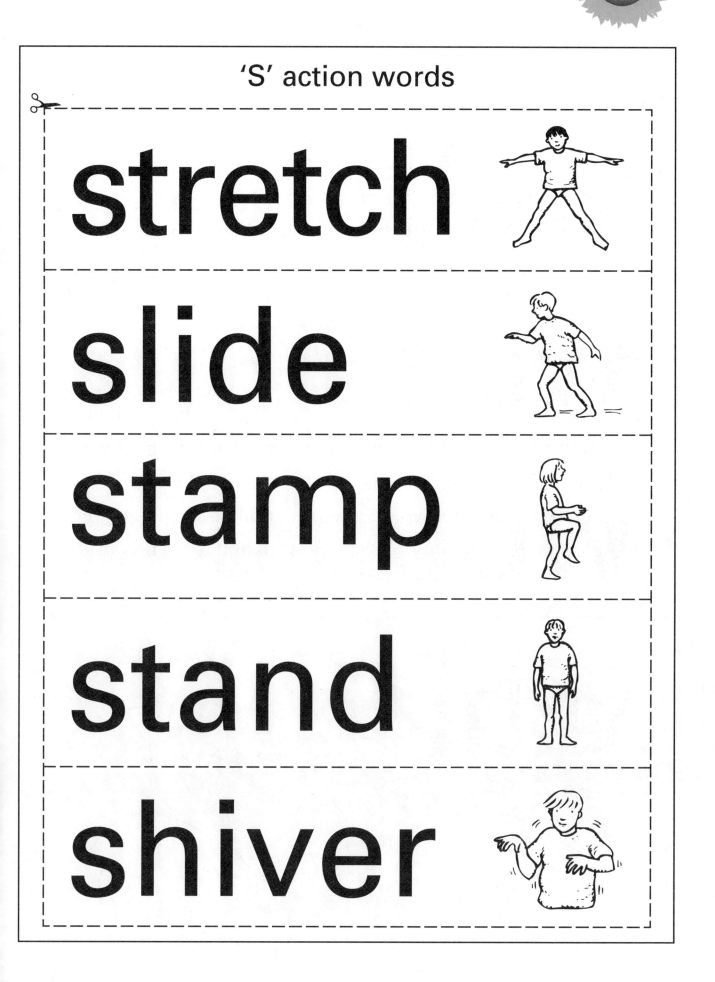

stretch

slide

stamp

stand

shiver

DANCE: *Under the sea*

PHOTOCOPIABLE   How do waves move on calm and stormy seas? Page 39 and Can we improve our representations of waves? Page 41

The Song of the Waves

We are the quiet, timid waves that gently kiss your toe.

We hardly seem to move at all, so softly do we flow.

The only sound we ever make is a whisper or a sigh,

But inch by inch we creep along until the tide is high.

We are the jolly, bubbling waves that laugh and splash with glee.

We bustle up the seashore, as merry as can be.

We spill our foam upon the beach, spread like a soapy pool,

Then slide back quickly to the sea and leave the hot sand cool.

We are the heavy, roaring waves, that burst in clouds of spray.

We crash against the cliff-side, and swirl and spin away.

As each of us falls backwards, there's another close behind

To hammer at the sturdy rocks; to smash and tear and grind.

Bernard W Martin

DANCE: **Under the sea**
How do small fish move? Page 42

PHOTOCOPIABLE

Fish

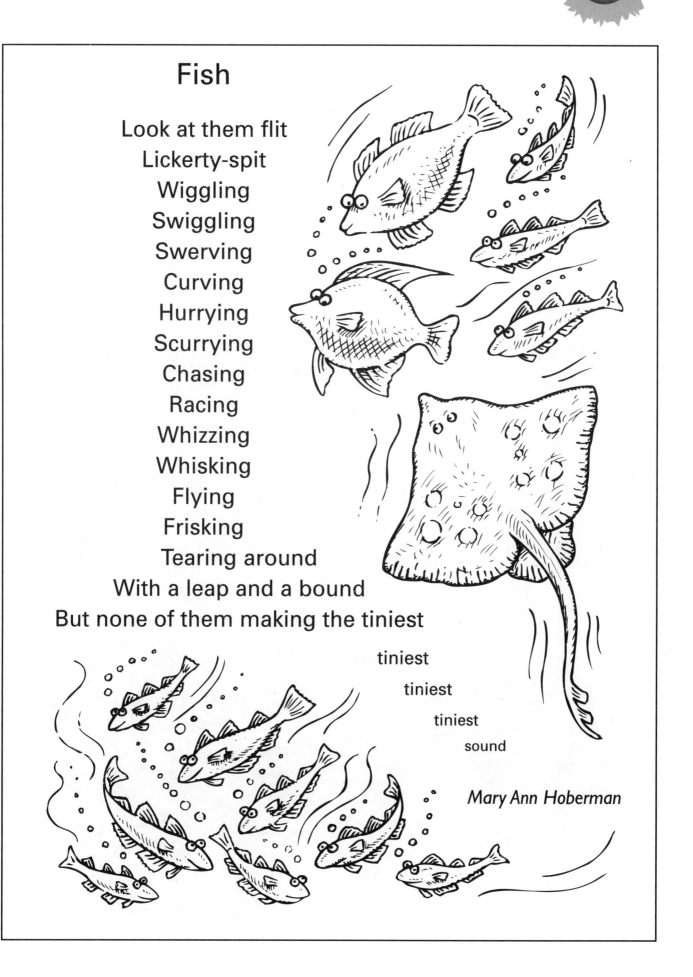

Look at them flit
Lickerty-spit
Wiggling
Swiggling
Swerving
Curving
Hurrying
Scurrying
Chasing
Racing
Whizzing
Whisking
Flying
Frisking
Tearing around
With a leap and a bound
But none of them making the tiniest

tiniest

tiniest

tiniest

sound

Mary Ann Hoberman

Under the Sea

Fish live under the sea
They dart, slide, glide,
Wave, bend, shoot,
Rush, twirl, weave and twist.
Whales live under the sea
They thrash majestically and propel
Water out of their spouts.
Crabs live under the sea
They scurry, scuttle,
Hide under the sand,
And move sideways.
Starfish live under the sea,
They have little holes under themselves.
Their five starfish arms
Cling on to the rocks.

Linda Christine Tubbage

DANCE: **Under the sea**
How do eels and sea snakes move? Page 45

PHOTOCOPIABLE

The Eel

The feel
of an eel
Is slippery,
Slimy;
He's sleek
And he's black as a panther
At night.
He slides
Through your fingers
Rapidly,
Slyly;
A flip
Of his tail
And he slips
Out of sight.

Robert S Oliver

DANCE: *Under the sea*
How do eels and sea snakes move? Page 45

PHOTOCOPIABLE

Sea Snake

Sea snake slipping through the water,
Black and white and black again;
Winding through the weeds of salt beds,
Hungry to inflict his pain.

Circling, seeking, wriggling by,
Silken movement, fixed – stare eye.
Deep fangs ready, small jaws part,
Paralysis of one small heart.

Coral Rumble

Travelling apparatus plan

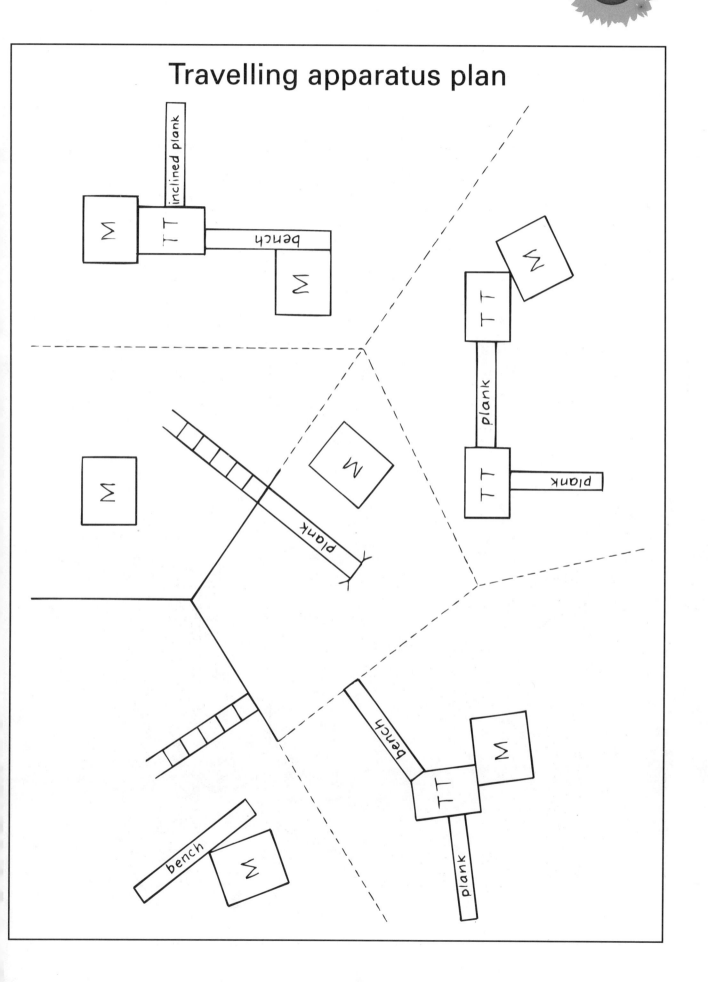

Balancing apparatus plan

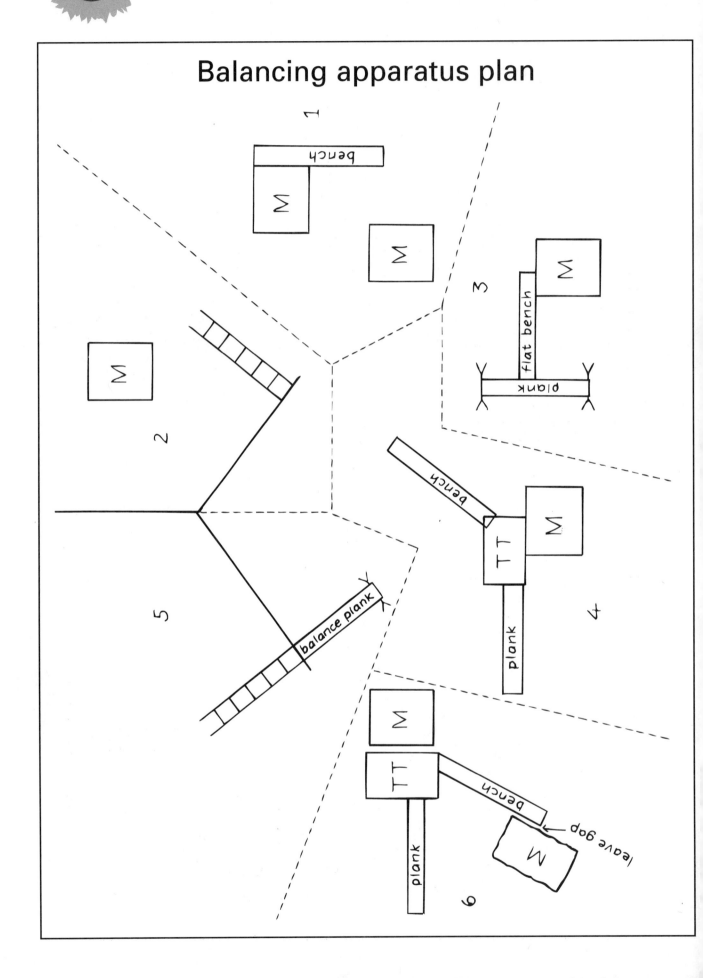

Pushing and pulling apparatus plan

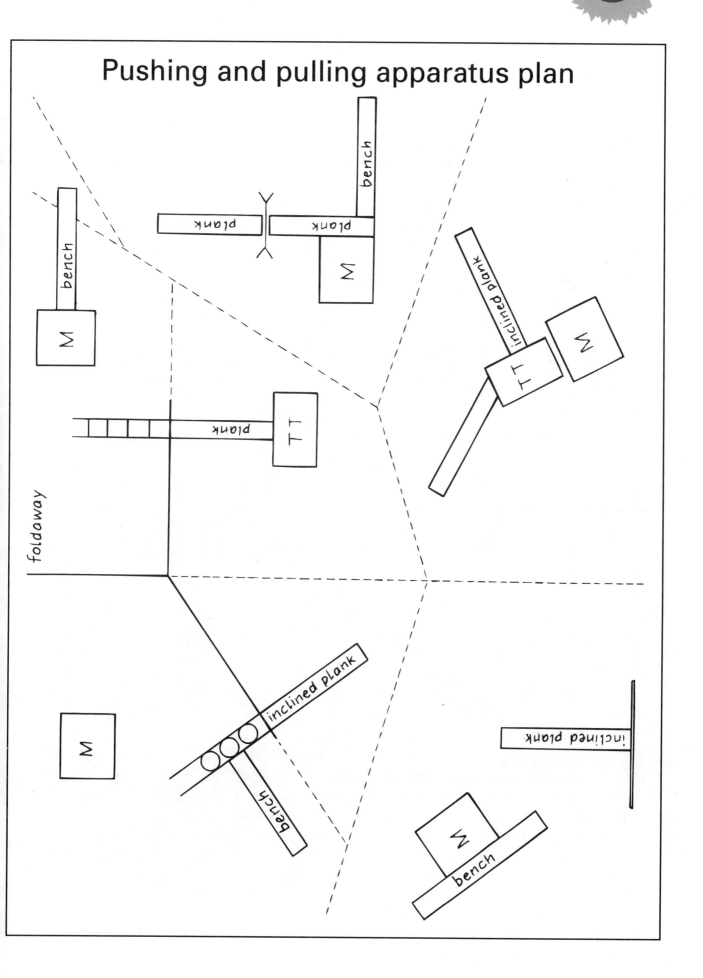

Warm-up and cool-down games (1)

Two, one, other
● Start with the children jogging in and out of the space.
● Give the instruction *Two*. The children are to touch the ground with *both* hands and then continue jogging.
● When you say *One*, they are to touch the ground with one hand and then continue jogging.
● When you say *Other*, they touch the ground with the hand they didn't use last time and then continue jogging.

The car game
● Children are to hold their ring like a steering wheel and jog in and out of all the spaces. They should stop still when you say *Stop*.
● *Stop* – brake and stop still.
● *Start* – move forward.
● *Change* – change direction.
● *Reverse* – move backwards.

Stop and go
● Begin with the children holding their ring like a steering wheel, moving around the space looking for spaces.
● *Stop* – put the ring on the floor and jog beside it.
● *Go* – pick the ring up and jog with it.
● *Reverse* – jog backwards holding the ring.

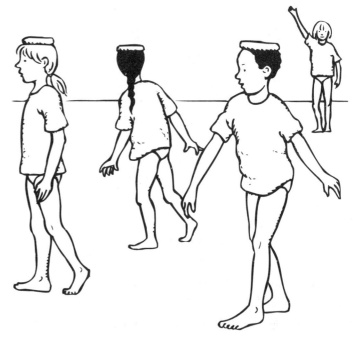

Help each other
● With a ring each on their heads, the children are to walk around using all the spaces, trying to keep their rings from falling off.
● If their ring falls to the floor, they stand still and put their hands up until someone comes to help them. They are not allowed to put the ring back themselves, but anyone else can pick it up and put it on their head for them.
● Everyone should look out for people needing help while they walk around.
● If someone helping loses their ring, then they wait for help too.

PRIMARY FOUNDATIONS: Physical education Ages 5–7

Warm-up and cool-down games (2)

Back to front
- The children need to be in pairs.
- One leads, jogging about the space, and the other follows.
- On the command *Back to front*, the person following sprints in front of their partner and becomes the leader.
- The new leader then slows to jogging and leads their partner in and out of the spaces, away from other pairs.
- There should be no crossing between the members of another pair.

Find your partner
- Each child should find a partner and shake hands.
- The children move away from each other into a new space.
- Everyone jogs in and out of everyone else, using all the space and keeping away from their partner.
- On a stop signal they are all to find their partners again and crouch down together in a space.
- Give the instruction to change partners and try again.

Follow my leader
- The children need to be in pairs.
- The leader explains or describes to their partner their first move (for example jumping with two feet together, hopping for three hops then changing legs), then demonstrates that action.
- The follower then joins in, copying their partner's actions.
- Give a signal to change over.

Warm-up and cool-down games (3)

Body parts
● Start with everyone walking about the space.
● Gradually increase the speed to jogging then running.
● Give a stop signal, either by using a whistle or your voice. The children should stop still like a statue.
● Say a part of the body (for example *Elbows*). The children must find a partner and touch elbows.
● Repeat using other parts of the body.

Jack Frost
● Choose four, five or six players to wear blue bands. These children are Jack Frost (the chasers).
● Choose a similar number of players to wear yellow bands (the sun).
● The rest of the children run around the space, chased by Jack Frost.
● When children are caught they are frozen and stand still (freeze) until they are released by a light touch on the arm by the the sun to defrost them.
● Once thawed, they can join in the game again and run around.
● Change roles until everyone has been either Jack Frost or the sun.

This way and that
● Begin with all the children in space, facing you.
● Point to your left and say *This way*. The children should all move to your left (their right).
● Point to your right and say *That way*. The children should move to their left.
● Alternate and speed up the directions.

Warm-up and cool-down games (4)

Side to side

● Start with the children in pairs, facing each other in plenty of space.
● One child moves from side to side and keeps changing direction after a few steps (not always the same number), suddenly stopping and starting.
● Their partner shadows them, trying to keep up and not letting them get more than two strides away.
● If, when you blow the whistle, the second child is close to their partner then they score a point. If their partner is more than two strides away then *they* get a point.
● Keep changing roles.

Chase the tail

● The children need to be in pairs. One child should have a band (tail) tucked into the back of their shorts.
● Give the instruction *Go*. The chaser's aim is to pull the tail from their partner. The child with the tail must then try and escape their chasing partner, keeping their tail out of reach.

Numbers

● Everyone jogs around the playground in and out of everyone else, looking for all the spaces.
● After a stop signal, say a number. The children have to get into groups of that number.
● You could finish with the exact number of the children in the class or in the group size they are to work in during the next task or activity.

Lifting and carrying apparatus

● Bend your knees, not your back to lift and lower.
● Walk.
● Face the direction in which the apparatus is being carried.
● Use both hands to lift and lower.
● Space yourselves out to spread the weight out evenly.

Mats: hold on with two hands.

Benches, planks and poles: position yourselves near each end and on each side near the middle; spread the weight out evenly between you.

Stools, trestle tables, box-tops and A-frames: carry using an undergrasp grip.